Brahms—The Vocal Music

Brahms—The Vocal Music

A. Craig Bell

Madison • Teaneck
Fairleigh Dickinson University Press
London: Associated University Presses

Associated University Presses
440 Forsgate Drive
Cranbury, NJ 08512

Associated University Presses
25 Sicilian Avenue
London WC1A 2QH, England

Associated University Presses
P.O. Box 338, Port Credit
Mississauga, Ontario
Canada L5G 4L8

The paper used in this publication meets the requirements
of the American National Standard for Permanence of Paper
for Printed Library Materials Z39.48-1984.

Library of Congress Cataloging-in-Publication Data

Bell, A. Craig.
    Brahms—the vocal music / A. Craig Bell.
        p.   cm.
    Includes catalog of vocal works and bibliographical references.
    ISBN 0-8386-3597-0 (alk. paper)
    1. Brahms, Johannes, 1833–1897.   Vocal music.   2. Vocal
music—19th century—History and criticism.   I. Title.
ML410.B8B38   1996
782.2'092—dc20   94-43514
                                                                              CIP
                                                                              MN

PRINTED IN THE UNITED STATES OF AMERICA

Contents

Preface

My reason for this study is quite simply a love and admiration of Brahm's songs and choral works going back over four decades, and this is accentuated by a sense of a lack of justice being accorded them by posterity—an injustice revealed by the recorded performance of over 150 of the lieder by Dietrich Fischer-Dieskau. This great lieder singer's consummate interpretations are a revelation as to the true stature of Brahms as a lieder composer, and should forever scotch the myth, perpetuated by some critics, that Brahms's range is less than that of Schumann and Wolf and surpassed only by that of Schubert.

Nor is it only the lieder that are so rarely performed. The *Requiem* excepted, how often are we given performances of such masterworks as the *Alto Rhapsody*, *Nänie*, and *Song of Destiny?**

Finally, two further points. (1) My aim throughout has been not to give dry technical analyses of the works as though they were some kind of extinct life to be examined under a critical microscope, but to attempt to illuminate and interpret.

(2) I have tried to integrate the songs into the different periods of the composer's life and so to make the book readable and to appeal both to professional and amateur musicians. If it introduces them to works they did not know, or reintroduces them to some they had all but forgotten, and if it succeeds in helping towards claiming a high place for Brahms among choral composers, I shall feel my attempt has been well worthwhile.

A. C. B.

*See Postlude for further discussion on the subject.

Brahms—The Vocal Music

Part I

1

Brahms and the Lied

By universal consent it is agreed that the Big Five of Song (using the term to mean art song in its widest sense) are Schubert, Schumann, Brahms, Wolf, and Fauré. Among them Schubert is the first, not only in chronology but in his range and fecundity, and also in the fact that he was the first composer to demonstrate to the world by a flood of miraculous examples that the setting of poetry to music could be an important sophisticated art form, a vital and urgent means of expression and not, as hitherto regarded, an occasional dilettante flirtation with social convention, a side issue and by-product.

Schumann followed in Schubert's wake to such a degree that it may not be an exaggeration to estimate his songs as the most imperishable of the offerings he has left to posterity. And despite some fine chamber and piano music and the Requiem, the same, I think, may be said of Fauré. Wolf is even easier to assess: for him the Lied was everything. If this cannot be said of Brahms it is merely because, like Schubert, he was a greater "all-rounder," and master of more musical forms than they were. Nevertheless, careful study of his almost two hundred songs tells us unequivocally that the Lied meant as much to him as it did to Schubert and his other compeers, and was not, as it was for Beethoven, Mendelssohn, and Strauss (to name only three composers who occasionally touched on greatness in the genre), a "part-time occupation," but rather a serious art form demanding a lifetime's devotion and study. His first and last works were songs.

Brahms was a descendant of Schubert, rather than of Schumann, whereas Wolf and Fauré are closer to the latter. Of course,

13

all songwriters owe something to Schubert as the first of the line, but broadly speaking the statement is true. This linking of Brahms with Schubert is based on (1) their attitude to the poetry they set and (2) the importance they accorded to the melodic line and the strophic form.

In this matter of choice of texts for setting, there is an aspect to consider that we tend to forget or overlook. The Germany of Schubert's time had no tradition of lyrical poetry for setting, such as English composers have been blessed with. There was no Shakespeare, no Herrick, no Burns, Blake, Byron, Moore, or Shelley to draw on. Goethe (1749–1832) was the first and greatest of the line, but apart from him and until the appearance of Heine (1797–1856) no lyrical poet of any stature existed: only a clutch of minor talent such as Müller, Claudius, Rellstab, Mayrhofer, Hölty, Platen—small links in the chain of German Romantic poetry whose effusions would in all probability have been totally forgotten but for Schubert's settings of them. Moreover, as bearers of the banner of nineteenth-century "romantic" *Schmalz*, their poems reek of morbidity, sentimentality, and self-pity, and teem with death-longings, outcast wanderers never able to find joy, rejected lovers endlessly weeping by streams, sending garlands to their beloveds bedewed with tears (*Tränen* along with *Herz* and *Schmerz* are to be found in almost every song), spending sleepless nights either wandering around the town or standing in streets yearning up at windows. Judged in the light of modern sentiment and literary criticism the poems that make up *Die schöne Müllerin*, *Winterreise*, *Dichterliebe*, and *Frauenliebe und Leben* are unmitigated *wershness*. But no critic, however clever he may think himself, can estimate contemporary art objectively and finally; and composers, who are in general nonliterary, are even less able to assess the quality of the poetry they set. If an indifferent poem happens to make a direct impact on his emotional palate and rhythmic sense, a composer will set it in preference to a better one that does not. So it was with Schubert and Brahms. In spite of being geniuses, they were still children of their age. They accepted that age's criteria as to what was worthwhile poetry and swallowed its emotionalism whole, having little else to set. If Brahms found that the poems of Daumer, Hölty, Candidus, and Groth gave him the initial springboard of inspiration better than those of Goethe or Mörike, why quarrel with that? The lesser poets gave him many masterpieces, the two latter between them a mere three. Let us not, therefore, be too censorious of their taste, but compensate by telling ourselves that by an inexplicable miracle, some magic alchemy, the dross of the texts has been transmuted into the pure gold of the music.

In any case, although Wolf contended that only "the best poetry" should claim the notice of the composer, others have stood out against his contention. Both Weber and Reger, for example, placed themselves in the opposite camp, maintaining that a truly great poem is whole, perfect, and complete in its own right, calling for no musical extension, and should be avoided by the composer who would do better to set less perfect poems that lent themselves better to their art. Almost the whole of Brahms's lieder and a good deal of Schubert's disproves Wolf's contention and sustains the Weber–Reger school of thought, just as the songs of Wolf (in general, but not always) and Fauré exemplify the former. That Brahms himself sided with the Weber–Reger school of thought is made clear by his words to the singer Henschel concerning Schubert, his ideal of a song composer. "Schubert's *Suleike* songs are for me the only instances where the strength and beauty of Goethe's words have been enhanced by the music. All the rest of Goethe's poems seem to me so perfect that no music can improve them."* No words could more clearly express the reason why the composer left Goethe and Heine practically alone and preferred to set minor poets.

There is also a further point to consider: who decrees what is to be adjudged "the best poetry"? The facile answer Posterity is not enough; for while it does sort the wheat from the chaff, it just as surely preserves the second and third rate along with "the best." For as Henry James observed, there is always a market for inferior goods, and the operettas of Sullivan and Offenbach appear to have every bit as good a prospect of survival as the operas of Handel, Gluck, Mozart, Verdi, and Wagner. In such cases immortality is rather like Orwell's equality: all are immortal, but some are more immortal than others. And this is because there is within the overall sanction of posterity a less permanent syndrome of taste or fashion that decrees that "the best" for one generation is often the worst for another. The status in the eyes

*G. Henschel, *Personal Recollections of Johannes Brahms* (Boston, 1907).

of successive generations of such poets as Donne, Keats, Shelley, Byron, and Tennyson, for example, and composers like Hummel and Spohr, reveal this dichotomy. The pendulum of taste swings violently and constantly, only coming to rest at the name of some universal genius who stands above aesthetic argument. Contemporary opinion of any artist can never be trusted and is always fallible, as the history of criticism shows.

This matter of literary taste, then, allied with the suitability or nonsuitability of poetry for musical setting, boils down surely to the old saw that has the practical wisdom of the ages behind it: The proof of the pudding is in the eating. In the end the composer must be the final judge, and his music will either vindicate or condemn him. All that matters, surely, is the quality of the result.

Let us consider now, briefly, the forms in which Brahms cast his songs. Like those of his compeers, the structures used by Brahms for his songs can be divided into three classifications: the simple strophic; the varied strophic; and the "durch-componiert," or "through-composed." It is interesting to consider the numerical balance of these within the total corpus of Brahms's work in this genre.

I stated earlier that Brahms linked himself with Schubert rather than the other great lieder composers, not only by being less critical of the poems he set, but also by his acceptance of the strophic form as a fully admissible musical expression of a poem. The critical head-shaking over this, while understandable, is far from being automatically valid. The form demands its own art no less than the more complex forms. Indeed, Brahms went so far as to declare that to compose melodies that would fit and bear the weight of every verse of a poem was infinitely more difficult than the other forms. This is in no small measure due to the fact that, being one of the greatest melodists, he saw in melody *per se* one of the pristine and most emotive elements in music—a fact that goes far in accounting for his love of folk music, and a factor to which I shall give attention later. Most folk song is strophic and the songs of Schubert and Brahms in strophic form, harmonized by each in his own style, are sophisticated extensions of it.

The criticisms leveled against strophic form are twofold: (1) it is mere repetition, sometimes to the point of monotony, and (2) the stanzas of any poem, particularly a long one, cannot possibly

be all in one identical mood and so cannot be adequately expressed by the same melody. In other words, the suggestion is
that the composer is taking the easy way out. There is some truth
in this criticism, and it is Schubert who leaves himself more
open to both charges. His sheer fecundity, allied with his easygoing nature and too-frequent lack of self-criticism, permitted
him to produce without a qualm such songs as *Die Spinnerin*,
Jägers Liebeslied, *Der Abend*, and *An die Freude*, to name but
four among many. In all these the same melody, itself not particularly distinguished, and an inordinate number of stanzas, can
only be characterized as monotonous to the point of tedium. It
may be argued, of course, that most of such songs were early and
immature; but the strophic mode clung to him to the end, though
in maturity it was more controlled, for example, *Frühlingssehn-
sucht* in *Schwanengesang* (1828), *Auf dem Wasser zu singen*
(1823), and even in so great a work as *Die schöne Müllerin*. It
cannot but be felt that the inartistically unfortunate juxtaposition of three slow strophic songs *Morgengruss*, *Des Müllers Blumen*, and *Tränenregen*, each with four verses, together with the
final song, *Des Baches Wiegenlied*, which has five, slows the
momentum and does not avoid a feeling of repetitiousness.

Brahms, more self-critical, was also much more careful, more
artistic, and more subtle in this matter. He ensured that the quality of the melody was such that it could bear the strain of repetition. Careful examination will show that the melodies are almost
invariably of the richest caliber, the most haunting quality. Along
with this he takes care (1) that the number of verses is limited,
never exceeding four, usually short, and (2) the mood of each
verse is similar, and so is adequately expressed by the same melody and harmony. Examples of these are, to name only a few,
Über die See, *Abschied*, *O liebliche Wangen*, *Klage (III)*, *Scheiden
und Meiden*, and *Das Mädchen spricht*. It may come as a surprise
to many to learn that the number of strophic songs is in fact
comparatively small in proportion to the total number,
amounting to not more than thirty-six out of the 196 included
in this survey, and of those thirty-six half, naturally and rightly,
are folk settings.

The sixty-odd through-composed songs, as would be expected,
are settings of longer poems that defy being broken down into
short strophes, and are mostly of an impassioned nature. Though
this type is to be found in all the stages of Brahms's career, the

majority occur in the later periods. Typical examples are *An eine Äolsharfe* (Op. 19, no. 5), *Wie rafft' ich mich auf in der Nacht* (Op. 32, no. 1), *Die Kränze* (Op. 46, no. 1), *Es träumte mir* (Op. 57, no. 3), *Der Tod, das ist die kühle Nacht* (Op. 96 no. 1), *Immer leise wird mein Schlummer* (Op. 105, no. 2).

Thus, simple arithmetic brings us face to face with the fact that the greatest number of songs, amounting to almost half the total, fall outside the two categories. This third type is not easy to define, and indeed I feel that a new term is needed for it in that, as regards Brahms, it is the most important and individual of the three. One may loosely describe it as "part strophic," "varied strophic," "strophic à la Brahms," or in some such terms; but it is elusive, often hovering vaguely between and sharing the form of the other categories, defying formal analysis. Such songs comprise many of his greatest and most typical, and constitute one of his most important and unique contributions to the Lied. In stating this, I am not claiming that he originated it. That honor goes to Schubert who used it occasionally (*Die Forelle; Gute Nacht,* from *Winterreise, Aufenthalt,* and *An der Mond (II)* are particularly good examples), but not to the same extent nor in the same manner as Brahms. Essentially it personifies the principle of variation in all its aspects—melodic, harmonic, and rhythmic.

Most of the great composers have written variations, and not a few have embodied some of their finest achievements in the form. But of them all, it is supremely in Haydn, Beethoven, and Brahms that what may be called the "instinct of variation" forms a guiding element from first to last. In saying this I do not have in mind only their variations so named, though such works as the "Andante Varié in F Minor," the "Diabelli," "Handel," "Haydn," and "Paganini" variations of these composers are among the most memorable of their kind. What is more important is the primal creative impulse, the whole mode of creation involved. Ernest Newman put his finger on it when he quoted Coleridge on Shakespeare: "He goes on creating and evolving B out of A, and C out of B, and so on, just as a serpent moves, which makes a fulcrum of its own body and seems for ever twisting and untwisting its own strength."* Newman was

*Ernest Newman, "Brahms and the Serpent" in *More Essays from the World of Music* (London: Calder, 1956).

describing Brahms's last piano works, but his remarks are just as pertinently applied to the songs. It is the problem, the ever-recurring, all-important problem of continuity that has to be solved, and one resolved only by the greatest masters, and not always even by them, as so many of the large-scale works of the Romantic composers only too clearly reveal. Hence their preference for the symphonic poem and the various shorter, lyrical forms less demanding of sustained architectonic thought. Not that—let adverse criticism say what it will—Brahms did not succeed with large-scale forms. The corpus of his chamber music alone proves as much. But on a general count it is with his last piano works and the songs that he comes nearest to perfection, and this because the whole problem reverts to the principle of which he was, with Haydn and Beethoven, the greatest master—that of variation. It is by the ever changing, mutable, incredibly varied transmutations of this themes that he turns simple, strophic songs into hybrid, protean forms full of subtle potency and nuance, impressing them with diversity within unity and unity within diversity, which gives them their unique character and strength.

The many ways in which Brahms does this can be seen by anyone who cares to study the songs. One of the most common is, with a three-verse poem, to make the first two verses strophic and then, while preserving the basic melodic, harmonic, and rhythmic structure, to vary the third verse in order to bring off a more telling climax. His very first song, *Liebestreu*, is a perfect example. Others are *Juche!*, *Treue Liebe*, *Komm bald*, *Herbstgefühl*, and *Blinde Kuh*. At other times, he will alter the middle verse and make the last a *reprise*, but add a brief coda, thus creating a simple ABA (e.g., *Wie die Wolke*, *Nachtigallen schwingen*, *Minnelied*, *Auf dem See (I)*, and *Botschaft*. If there are only two verses, he will vary the second (e.g. *Magyarisch*, *An ein Veilchen*, *Ach, wende diesen Blick*, and *Sapphishe Ode*). Or yet again he will make a rondo of it, as with *Frühlingstrost*, *Erinnerung*, and *An die Tauben*. Other devices are to make one strophe major and the other minor, and vice versa, or, while retaining the same melody throughout, to vary the accompaniment. He can make the references to previous phases so elusive and subtle that one is in doubt whether they are strophic à la Brahms or through-composed (e.g., *Mein wundes Herz*; *Geh-*

eimnis; Willst du, dass ich geh?; Auf dem See (II); Verrat; and
Todessehnen). And one of the most beautiful and best-known of
songs, the op. 105, no. 1 *Wie Melodien zieht es mir,* as singers
trying to memorize it know to their cost, is also one of the most
cunningly varied, in that while each of the three verses begins
with the same melody, each of the middle sections is different,
giving greater nuance to the words.

Allied with Brahms's genius for melodic and harmonic variation is another facet in which he is generally acknowledged as
the master of masters: that of rhythm, or, more strictly, rhythmic
variation. This stems partly from his deliberately acquired and
hard-earned contrapuntal skill won by his lifelong study of Bach
and Handel and the pre–Baroque masters, but chiefly, like all
such powers, from the inexplicable workings of natural genius.
His notorious rhythmical complexities, disjunctions, disloca-
tions—call them what you will—are miracles of skill beyond all
analysis, and are achieved with the apparent ease and mastery
of legerdemain. The methods used are astoundingly varied and
provide evidence of staggering craftsmanship. Overlapping
phrases, cross rhythms, syncopation, imitation, two beats against
three, six against four, change of beat in the middle of a measure,
combinations of phrases of different lengths, melodic lines combining at different tempi, 4-beat phrases stretching across 3-beat
bars, and shortening and lengthening of phrases are among the
methods he employs to give endless variety to his melodies and
to the pulse of the music. Examples occur in almost every one
of his instrumental works from the earliest to the last, especially
in his chamber music, as pianists, violinists, violists, and cellists
know only too well, meeting time and time again as they do those
fearsome passages in which each one of them is playing against
the rest—passages that on paper often seem unnecessarily difficult and complex but that, once mastered, sound inevitably right.

It would be strange if the instrumental Brahms did not bring
these same characteristics into his vocal works; and indeed we
find similar rhythmic flexuous convulsions there between melody and harmony, and between the vocal line and the accompaniment, time and time again. His very first published song,
Liebestreu (Op. 3 no. 1) is a revel of cross-rhythm not only between the pianist's two hands but also between them and the
voice, together with devices such as imitation and overlapping
phrases; and it must have been the technical mastery together

with the sheer emotive power of the song that so roused the admiration of Joachim and the Schumanns. It is the rhythmic surge and a cross-beat of the piano against the voice that gives *Frühlingstrost* its headlong impetus. In the comparatively simple *Errinerung*, the original elementary chordal accompaniment becomes varied with each return of the theme. *Lerchengesang*, one of the composer's supreme songs, has one of the subtlest accompaniments in all lieder, blending a rhythm of eight quavers per measure with a vocal line consisting of tripled-crotchets. The strophic, folklike melody of *Ade!* is sung over a ferociously fast and complex accompaniment in which the sextuplet semiquavers of the right hand are opposed by triplet quavers in the left. Like the slow movement of the Op. 101, C Minor piano trio, *Agnes* has a time signature of 3/4/2/4. The second version of *Beim Abschied*, in which a 3/8 vocal line is heard over a 2/4 accompaniment throughout, is a tour de force of rhythmic ingenuity. *Frühlingslied* (Op. 85, no. 5) is one of the most dauntingly complex of all, the three lines seeming to have nothing to do with one another. The melody, itself unusual in that it is full of un—Brahms-like intervals such as major 7ths and diminished 4ths, is set to an onrushing accompaniment, the right hand consisting of broken 4-beat quavers with snippets of imitation of the voice and leaping syncopations, all against a near *moto perpetuo* of triplet quavers in the left hand.

Ex. 1 Frühlingslied

Though only three pages in length, the song is so intense and complex that only a singer and pianist with high levels of technique, plus a sense of togetherness born of practice and affinity, can hope to put the song together to make it sound as the composer imagined it, that is, a perfect ensemble and meaningful interpretation of Geibel's poem of hope for the spring about to break the numbing spell of winter, overflowing with zest and rapture.

One might go on citing examples endlessly; but I have surely given sufficient convincing illustration to show why Brahms is one of the greatest masters of lieder, and that his unique contribution to the art song lies chiefly in his manipulation of the varied strophic form, together with a miraculous blend of melody, and harmonic and rhythmical originality.

Of his purely melodic genius and the influence on it of folksong, I shall have more to say later. To conclude this introductory general chapter I will merely add that, as for his great lieder compeers Schubert, Schumann, and Wolf, for Brahms the art song was a mode of expression of primary importance. His songs allow us intimate glimpses into his technical workshop and his development, along with disclosures of his philosophy concerning human life, its hopes, frustrations, and, at times, stark tragedy. His songs are not only a concentration of melodic impulse and harmonic intensity and variation, but a revelation of a deeply meditative, speculative mind. In them he found his most personal and perfect means of self-expression. And for the present writer at least, it is by his chamber music, variations, last piano works, and above all, by his songs, that Brahms places himself beyond dispute alongside the greatest masters.

2

The Early Songs

Brahms's first songs were published in three sets of six as Op. 3, 6, and 7, Op. 3 and Op. 7 in 1854, Op. 6 in 1853. All, except the earliest extant song, *Heimkehr* (Op. 7, no. 6, dating from 1851) were composed in 1852 and 1853, and I propose to treat them collectively. To call them juvenilia would be wrong, though the composer was barely twenty when he wrote them. In the first place, one has the feeling that Brahms was never really young in the sense that Schubert, Beethoven, or Mozart were. In the second, he was so self-critical, destroying so many works and preserving only those that completely satisfied him, often with long-delayed revisions, that one hesitates to characterize any work of his as youthful. Even those songs that are the least mature and representative do not have that gap of style and technique between them and the later ones that is so apparent in the first works of Schubert, Wolf, and Fauré. Thus, while only three of these eighteen songs can be described as mature, the rest are by no means negligible, and remain of interest as examples of the composer's struggles towards finding himself. The three outstanding songs are *Treue Liebe* (Op. 7, no. 1), *Wie die Wolke* (Op. 6, no. 5), and *Liebestreu* (Op. 3, no. 1). The first is a setting of a poem that is typical of the fustian turned out by the minor, and sometimes even major, German poets of the nineteenth century—in this instance Ferrand, a pseudonym for Eduard Schulz. A young woman sits at the edge of the sea yearning for her absent lover. She allows the tide to engulf her. Her vigil is over: she has found him. The young romantic Brahms found in this farrago of melodrama all the stimulus needed in a poem for a composer to feel the urge to set it, be its literary quality what it may—rhythm, evocation, the power of suggestion, description (enabling him to paint a scene), and a single unified idea. It gave him, in fact, a picture, a scene of desolation, absence, and love faithful to death—three attributes that remained dear to him all his life— and the combination moved him to create a splendid song. The wistful F♯-minor melody is sustained by rising and falling arpeggios, suggestive of the lapping waves, and perhaps, to romantic imagination, the sad voices of drowned sailors calling irresistibly to the forlorn girl.

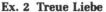

Ex. 2 Treue Liebe

As the waves surge round her, the accompaniment figurations break into triplets and become agitated, while the vocal line rises to its climax on the words "Tiefe mit stiller Gewalt," after which the arpeggios subside, the voice intones a quasi-recitative of heartbreak, and the postlude takes the music lower and lower as though dragging life and hope into the depths. In addition to the song's intrinsic merit, it is also a fine example of Brahms's treatment of strophic form, the final verse being reshaped to bring out the romantic climax.

Wie die Wolke must be saluted as the first of the many magnificent love songs to come. This, in its idealism, warmth, and tenderness, places itself alongside the lyrical masterpieces of Schumann. "As the clouds, the sunflower, and the eagle all turn toward the sun, so I turn to you for my deepest joy" is the gist of Fallesleben's poem. The accompaniment, as though spellbound by the beauty of the melodic line, echoes it in off-beat sixths, the left hand suggesting faint horn calls from far-off vistas. In bars six and seven the piano doubles the melody. An unexpected shift through A major into F♯ major, together with the *dim. e sost.* at "sterbend ihr am Busen hangt," catch tonally all the visual beauty engendered by the words. In the third stanza, the simile of the eagle takes the music into the tonic minor, where the climactic passage describing the fall of the eagle to earth ("blind zur Erde nieder fallt") by a chromatic descent from high G accentuated by unisons in the bass, is a touch of sheer magic and pictorial imagination in which the moment of truth blazes out, declaring the appearance of the successor to Schumann. The final stanza makes a return to the melody and major key of the first but—and note the mature subtlety of the young composer here—with the accompaniment given to the *minore* episode. The song is gloriously crowned by a codetta of wistful, transcendent beauty in the repeat of the final phrase of the poem, "und an ihren Glanz vergehn."

Ex. 3 Wie die Wolke

The song is without prelude or postlude, a fact that occurs only seven times in the whole output of the lieder. But let no one venture criticism in this instance. The final "vergehn," murmured like an incantation above the piano's B-major chords, is as eloquent as any postlude.

Liebestreu was composed in January of 1853, and therefore after most of the songs in Op. 6 and Op. 7 although it appeared as the first song in the composer's earliest published set, thought

by the composer to be worthy of dedication to that remarkable
woman Bettina von Armin, friend of Joachim and the Schumanns
and correspondent with Beethoven. This was the work over and
above the rest that made Joachim and the Schumanns see in
the young genius "he who is to come" in Schumann's famous
proclamation. The song is one of those dialogues between
mother and daughter that are so common in German poetry. Here
the mother tells her daughter to tear her love-grief from her heart;
to sink it in the sea like a stone; to pluck it out like a withered
blossom; to throw it to the wind like a leaf. But the girl replies
that her advice is useless: the stone will lie on the bed of the
sea, the blossom will bloom again, and the wind, though it may
wear away rock, cannot wear out her immutable love. The E-flat
minor key signature, one of Brahm's tragic keys, *sehr langsam*,
and *p con espressione* warn the singer and pianist in advance
that this is to be a deeply felt song. And in fact it proves to be a
masterpiece in every way—in interpretation of the poem, in-
formal shaping, in its melodic line, and in its harmonic strength.
All the fingerprints of the mature Brahms are here: the *agitato*
right hand sextuplets throbbing in cross-rhythm against a hollow,
persistent bass figuration, canonically anticipating and overlapping the mother's interjections; and the shifting of the pianist's
left hand from the low bass for the mother to the unison treble
for the girl, thus giving each her distinct character.

Ex. 4 Liebestreu

The first two verses are strophic, but for the final verse the music blazes into a climactic major, after which the song dies mournfully away to a pianissimo close. Over and above its maturity, astonishing for a composer of twenty, the song is a perfect illustration of Brahms's genius even then for combining romantic *Angst* with classical control. The excited admiration of Joachim and Schumann on first hearing it is easily understood. The lied is to Brahms much as *Gretchen am Spinnrade* is to Schubert— a moment of time in which the psychic atoms of inspiration combined to draw from the young composer a masterpiece that stood out above all his coeval works and looked far into the future. In short, the song proclaims a future master of the Lied.

A word of warning to the singer here. Only a soprano with a voice adequate for the climax and the ability to express profound emotion *mezza voce* should attempt this testing song. In fact, I cannot help thinking that Brahms made a miscalculation in setting the *tessitura* so high—a belief supported by the fact that the song is more often performed transposed by mezzo sopranos and even contraltos. The reason is clear: the song needs the more full-bodied timbre of the lower voice—in which case the pianist in his delight in the intricate cross rhythms and impassioned sonorities must take care not to overwhelm the singer at the climax.

Against the mature perfection of these three songs the remainder can only seem comparatively pale reflections. Nevertheless, although full of immaturities and echoes of the young composer's more immediate influences—Schubert, Schumann, Mendelssohn, and Franz—they never fall below a reasonable level and are by no means all dispensable. *Liebe und Frühling (I)* is a naive setting of a poem by Fallersleben proclaiming the return of love along with the spring to a young man's heart. The accompaniment is mostly in unison with the voice, though there is a brief hint of counterpoint at the *poco piu lento*, where the voice sings the opening phrase of the melody in augmentation while the piano plays its own countermelody—a hint of the Brahms to come.

Liebe und Frühling (II) with its text by the same poet, is in effect an extension of the previous song. The beloved herself, the poet declares, is the spring, which without her would be meaningless. The music, while being more expansive, reveals still more the influence of Schumann.

Lied, a setting of Bodenstedt, has a Russian background. A girl watching a seagull hovering over the Volga and an eagle wheeling over the steppe sees in their unwary prey an epitome of her own betrayed heart and calls on heaven and earth to end her misery. Brahms gives the poem a turbulent E-flat minor setting, and the first four bars of each verse (the song is strophic plus a coda) with their impassioned rise and fall in a splendid arch of sound arouse expectations of greatness. But partly, I think, because the various images of the overlong poem tend to weaken the impact of the girl's despair, the music falls off in quality; and the blazing climax of the *ff* coda seems too operatic as an expression of a young girl's grief.

The pensive little *In der Fremde* would have been a welcome setting of Eichendorff's poem had not Schumann immortalized it fifteen years earlier as the first song of his Op. 39 *Liederkreis* cycle. The influence of the elder composer's setting (down to the same key of F minor and identical variations in the text) is too pronounced to let Brahms's version stand in its own right.

The last song of the set, like the fourth, entitled *Lied*, is also a setting of Eichendorff, and has the same theme of homesickness. Its four verses are set AABA, with a varied accompaniment for the final reprise and coda—a form later to give us so many great songs. Here, however, in the F-major "B" episode, the music loses impetus, and the return to the tonic A major gives an impression of contrivance.

Every singer and lover of lieder knows Wolf's *In dem Schatten meiner Locken*, but how many of them, one wonders, are aware that the *Spanisches Lied* which opens Brahms's Op. 6, is also a setting of the same Heyse poem? In art as in sport it is the fate, often unjust, of the also-rans to be eclipsed by the winners. Had it not been for Schubert's *Erlkönig*, Loewe's setting would have been better known today, for it is an effective song, and but for Wolf's famed setting this song of Brahms's would be better appreciated. The Spanish color and atmosphere are aptly caught by the rhythms of the accompaniment, as too are the changes in the girl's mood as she watches over her sleeping lover by a hesitant triplet arpeggio leading into the alternating major episodes.

Ex. 5 Spanisches Lied

While it may not be the equal of the Wolf setting, nevertheless the number of songs written specifically for women being few as against those for men, I do not hesitate to suggest that this of Brahms is well worth attention, for it can be made an attractive song if performed with the requisite art by singer and all-important pianist.

Der Frühling and *Juche!* pair themselves by reason of their mood, being settings of poems rare in the annals of Romantic poetry—poems proclaiming that the world is a beautiful place and that man and nature and art should combine to express that truth. The young and still hopeful Brahms leaped to the message, and none of his songs surpasses these in zest and exuberance. The first is a welcome to spring and all the hope and beauty it brings with it. The verve of the pulsating eight-bar prelude sets the tone, and the interruptions in the vocal line express an almost breathless rapture above an accompaniment of dancing triplet quavers. It is to be regretted that at this early stage the young composer's technical equipment was not always adequate to sustain the initial inspiration. Variation is needed, whereas the song is simple strophic, and by the third verse the pristine magic has lost something of its power; nor is this quite restored by the thirteen-bar postlude (the longest incidentally, in all his songs) which, after an exciting, upward-surging *crescendo*, loses impetus by falling to a p *dolce* and slower tempo in the mid-regions of the piano.

Juche! likewise expresses unconfined joy, but again repetition and lack of variety must be the main criticism. Yet immature as both these songs are, singers might do worse than bear them in mind as happy contrast to the more usual sombre tones and slow tempi, and the pianist will revel in the brilliant fast-moving accompaniments.

Nachwirkung, the least satisfactory of these eighteen songs, attempts to set a poem consisting entirely of feminine rhymes, always difficult for a composer, and Brahms fails, much as Schubert failed, with his *In der Ferne*. Schubert did at least vary his strophes, whereas Brahms simply repeats them, with resultant monotony.

The last of the set, *Nachtigallen schwingen*, is, with the exception of the trio already singled out, the best. This impassioned song is full of the mature composer's fingerprints: the enharmonic modulation (C♭ = B) for the middle strophe with its syncopations and cross-rhythms; the variation in the accompaniment for the final strophe when the left hand, instead of doubling the right as in the first, unexpectedly climbs smoothly from the bass up into the treble regions with an expressive cello-like effect; the inspiration of the interjected bar at "traurig sinnend still"; and the cadence for the final "die nicht blühen will." The only criticism might be that among the joyous nightingales and burgeoning blossoms the contrasting grief of the lone lover is not sufficiently caught by the music. All the same, if the song is not among the supreme greats of the mature Brahms, it deserves to be in the repertoire of all self-respecting lieder singers.

Of the six songs of Op. 7, I have already discussed the outstanding *Treue Liebe*. The second, *Parole*, is full of horn calls suggesting the huntsman who is the object of the girl's love. Perhaps because it is one of the earliest (1852), it is imitative almost to the point of being plagiaristic in its middle section (its form is ternary), where Schubert's *Rückblick* is all but quoted. No doubt Brahms would have thrown his famous "Any idiot can see that!" in the face of anyone having the temerity to draw his attention to the fact. And indeed, if one overlooks this, it is a most attractive song, with a climax that should make it appeal to a good tenor.

Anklänge is something of a problem. The poem, taken from the *Gedichte* of Eichendorff, seems inconclusive and out of place as a separate entity, its eight lines simply describing a girl sitting in the twilight in a lonely house on the mountain side, spinning her wedding dress. No emotion and no personality are suggested. It is merely a static scene. We do not know whether the girl is happy or unhappy. The poem has no mood, no color. What was a composer to make of it? What did Brahms see in it to make him set it? Whatever the impetus might have been, the music is bafflingly enigmatic, even, at first hearing, neutral. But upon repetition one becomes aware that the minor key, the *mezza voce* vocal line, and the octave syncopations of the right hand above a lugubrious bass of thirds whose top notes form a hollow-sounding unison with the voice, invoke an atmosphere of sadness and foreboding; and though the second strophe is brightened by a higher and more lightly harmonized bass, and the postlude closes unexpectedly on a major chord, the repetition of the last two lines of the poem with reiterated low A's in the bass does little to contradict the overall sense of melancholy. Whatever might have been the poet's meaning, Brahms, one senses, intends us to feel the girl will never wear her wedding dress

The sixth song, *Heimkehr*, is the earliest of Brahms's published songs, being written as early as 1851. That he allowed it to go undestroyed when so many others were thrown into his wastepaper basket is a testimony to its quality. Its mere twenty-one bars, making it one of the shortest songs ever written, have the strength of the bridge, the rock and the earth that the homecomer of Uhland's poem invokes to stay inviolable until he and his beloved meet again. The prelude's strident, upward-leaping phrases in the right hand, anticipating those of the voice and to be repeated almost menacingly in the bass, give a satisfying unity of form. Brief though the song is, it contains subtle points that its fast tempo and terseness may cause to be overlooked on a single hearing: imitation between voice and piano bass (bars 15—

18); and cross-rhythm in the piano (bars 12 and 13). The song ends with a thrice-repeated "bis ich mag bei der Liebsten sein" in a magnificent *ff* climax in the major.

To round off my survey of these examples of Brahms's early essays in the genre in which he was to become one of the greatest masters, I draw the reader's attention to an extraneous song without opus number that, though composed at this time (1853) but deliberately withheld from publication until 1872, is too attractive to be passed over without mention merely because, like *In der Fremde*, it duplicates one of Schumann's finest and most celebrated songs. This is no less than a setting of Eichendorff's *Mondnacht*. If, as seems probably, Brahms held it back for fear odious comparisons might be made between it and Schumann's setting, his fears were groundless. Wonderful as the latter's song is, that of the younger composer is no less exquisite. With its *Träumerisch* atmospheric prelude so subtly anticipating the melodic line's *pp* echo at bars 27–30, the voice's dreamy melody sung through a gently rocking accompaniment full of ravishing enharmonic modulations, above all its ethereal fade-away over a pedal A♭, it succeeds no less in capturing the ecstatic peace and beauty of the poem, and would be no anticlimax if sung after the Schumann masterpiece. Lieder singers—note!

Following the publication of the previous three groups of songs, a gap of seven and eight years respectively ensued before Brahms published his next two song collections as Op. 14 and Op. 19, and even then these were to consist of no more than thirteen original songs, of which seven were settings of folk-poems.

The reasons not only for the paucity of lieder but of published compositions of any kind over this period become clear if we consider the pressures of his life. The years 1853–6, and even later, were a period of sheer tragedy for the composer and the man—a traumatic memory he was never to forget or even completely to put behind him and which, it is not I think too much to say, began the transformation of his whole character. To begin with—Schumann. It was in the February of 1853 that, after showing symptoms of behavior approaching madness during which he imagined he had received themes from the spirits of Schubert and Mendelssohn, he tried to kill himself by throwing himself into the Rhine. He was pulled out in time, only to spend the three years of life left to him in an asylum. His wife, Clara, then 35 and pregnant with her son Felix, was almost driven out of her mind. On hearing the news, Brahms, then at Hanover, hurried to Düsseldorf, and sacrificing everything, made the town his home in order to be near her and to give her and her large family all the comfort and help he could. As time passed and intimacy increased, the young composer's feelings towards Clara changed from those of friendship, affection, and admiration to love. Understanding this, faithful to the memory of her adored husband, and harassed by the inevitable cares of a mother and housewife superimposed upon her career as one of the most famous professional pianists of her day, she was finally driven to separating herself and her family from him. But his love for her, though offset by absence, time, and ephemeral affairs with other women, remained a part of himself all his life, and this, allied with his passion for independence and belief that marriage would mean the loss of it, made him avoid all domestic ties and explains his indefensible retreat from other affairs such as Bertha Faber, Elizabeth Herzogenberg, Hermine Spies, and Alice Barbi—all singers.

Along with this tragic background went another reason for the scarcity of published work during this period. Schumann had said of him: "If he will only touch with his magic wand those massive forces of chorus and orchestra, and compel them to bequeath him their powers, we may expect still more wondrous glimpses of the spirit world."* The young composer was now to take Schumann at his word, and between 1854 and 1858, although he did not altogether forsake smaller piano works (see the "Schumann" variations, Op. 9; the four Ballades, Op. 10; and the two sets of variations, Op. 21), the greater part of his energies went into the production of large-scale compositions, and this meant slow and laborious work. There was too another factor. Of the eight *Songs and Romances* which comprise op. 14, all, with the exception of one—and that is thirteenth century—are settings of traditional texts. In other words, Brahms had come under the spell of folk song.

This, then, I think, is the appropriate time and place to exam-

*Schumann article "New Paths" (1853)

ine this aspect of his lieder, being as it was one of the most seminal sources of his art.

It may be asked: Why was it that of all the great creators of lieder, Brahms was the only one to devote himself so completely to the Volkslied, to feel for it a veritable passion that gripped him and influenced him from his first days to his last? The answer is, I think, twofold. As I have already stated, Brahms was one of the greatest of melodists. For him, as for Handel, melody was one of the pristine and most potent emotive forces of music. Both his instrumental and vocal works, filled as they are with those characteristic long melodic spans, are proof of this.

Ex. 6 First movement of Piano Trio, Op. 8

Ex. 7 Andante of Piano Quartet, Op. 60

Ex. 8 The Song *Wie Melodien zieht es mir*, Op. 105

Ex. 9 The Song *Sapphische Ode*, Op. 94

There can be no doubt but that in folk tune Brahms found the apotheosis of his love of melody. In fact, he was once heard to declare half jocularly that whenever he was in need of a melody he thought of a folk song. In other words, between him and folk melody was an innate affinity that no self-conscious imitation can replace and without which no genuine inspiration can be felt. A new world of music had been opened up for him, and he absorbed its atmosphere to such a degree that it became a part of him to the end of his composing life.

Additionally, in the late eighteenth and early nineteenth centuries Europe had witnessed an upsurge of nationalistic feeling expressed in the publication of folk poetry, ballads, and songs. Britain had been first in the field with the epoch-making Percy's *Reliques of Ancient English Poetry* (1765), with its profound effects on British literature. This was followed first by Herder's *Stimmen der Volker in Liedern* (1778–9), then by the historic Arnim-Brentano *Des Knaben Wunderhorn* (1808), and finally, by the much later (1840) *Deutsche Volkslieder mit ihren Original-Weisen* of Zuccalmaglio. Although the earlier collections had been available to him, their implications had been ignored by Schubert; and in fact prior to Brahms only Weber, Schumann, Mendelssohn, and Franz had dipped their buckets—and then only tentatively—into those fruitful wells. Brahms himself was not drawn to them either, for he used Herder for only one solo song and two duets, and the *Wunderhorn* for only two solo songs, two duets, and two part-songs. But he more than made up for this by his constant drawing on his favorite collection—the Zuccalmaglio. In these national melodies, Brahms, German to the core almost to the verge of chauvinism, quite apart from his innate love of them, saw a means of spreading his nation's folk songs not only throughout Germany but the world. He set himself to work on this labor of love, and the first fruits of it were the *Volks-Kinderlieder*, arranged for and dedicated to the children of Robert and Clara Schumann. These, written mostly in 1856 and 1857, consisted of no less than forty-two songs; but for reasons not altogether clear they were published in two volumes, the first anonymously in 1858 and including fourteen of the songs; the second, containing the remainder, posthumously in 1926 as twenty-eight *Deutsche Volkslieder*. From now on, folk-song arranging became a passion, almost an obsession with him, culminating in the famous forty-nine *Deutsche Volkslieder*, published in six volumes only three years before his death. Thus it was that, on the publication of this work, intending it to be his last, he wrote to his publisher Simrock: "Has it struck you that as a composer I have really taken my farewell? The last of the folk songs and the same air in my Op. 1 are like the serpent biting its own tail, and symbolise nicely that the story is finished."*

*Letter from Brahms to Simrock, 1891.

In a chapter such as this, devoted solely to the original lieder, it is not within my scope or purpose to examine his folk-melody arrangements, but only to refer to them inasmuch as their influence extends to the original songs. But there are two aspects of these arrangements that need to be mentioned because they have important repercussions on his lieder. The first is this: study of the former makes it apparent that in his first essays (see the *Volks-Kinderlieder*) the accompaniments are simple, sometimes to the point of naiveté. Certainly this comported with the melodies themselves and with the fact that they were made with children in mind; though whether this was done with deliberate intention or from timidity is uncertain. The fact that he did not put his name to the publication suggests that he might have had doubts as to their merit. But as he went on quietly collecting and selecting from the Zuccalmaglio collection (and indeed not only from German texts but translations from the Slavonic, Persian, Magyar, Scottish, Italian, and Spanish), and as his own music matured, his accompaniments became bolder, more independent, and characteristic. One has only to compare typical examples from the earlier collections with almost any of the forty-nine *Deutsche Volkslieder* to see the difference in approach. The latter have all the fingerprints of his original lieder accompaniments, and like them never, however independent they may be, obscure the pristine simplicity of the folk melody. In this respect, examples such as *Guten Abend* (No. 4), *Schwesterlein* (No. 15), *All mein Gedanken* (No. 30), *Es wohnet ein Fiedler* (No. 36), and *In stiller Nacht* (No. 42), to name only five, are models of the arranger's art. *In stiller Nacht*, perhaps the most famous of all, is not only the crowning glory of the collection, but in its rhythmic displacement serves as one of the best examples of his virtuosity and originality in cross-beat phrasing.

Ex. 10 *In stiller Nacht*

Study of his ninety folk-song arrangements proclaims Brahms to be along with Bartok the greatest in this field both in quantity and quality, with Vaughan Williams in honorable second place.

The second important aspect of these arrangements is that, induced by them to immerse himself deeper and deeper in folk-verse, Brahms was led to making his own settings of poems, and in these the same development from simplicity to complexity and a more individual voice is to be observed. His first attempts were the *Volkslied* and *Die Trauernde* (Op. 7, nos. 4 and 5), both plaintive little songs in a minor key, in which a girl laments her lonely, loveless fate. The accompaniments are very simple, with the right hand duplicating the melody, the first harmonized diatonically, the second by bleak modal triads revealing the young composer's knowledge of pre–Baroque music. Then, coming to the eight *Romances and Songs* of Op. 14, composed six or seven years later, we find that almost all are folk-verse settings, of which the best show both in their melodic line and accompaniments a more advanced and original treatment, making them recognizable for the first time as authentic Brahms. The first song, *Vor dem Fenster*, taken from Karl Simrock's 1851 collection *Die deutschen Volkslieder*, tells of the farewell of two lovers at the girl's window. The Romeo-Juliet situation, the intensity and pa-

thos of the young lovers is beautifully caught by Brahms in the
flowing 3/8 quavers of the melody, warmly harmonized in sixths
and thirds, with short but eloquent interruptions filled by the
piano as though the lovers ran out of words in their grief, while
the alternating minor-major strophes and Schubertian modulations give not only variety but poignant expressiveness to each
of the singers.

For *Murrays Ermordung* Brahms went to Herder's translation
of the well-known Scots ballad *The Bonny Earl of Murray*, and
it is interesting to compare Brahms's version with the traditional
folk melody. The tempo of the latter is slow, and the song, elegiac
rather than dramatic, concentrates on the grief to all who loved
him caused by Murray's murder at the hands of Huntley.
Brahms's song, *forte* and *con moto*, on the other hand seems to
seethe with violence and rage at the wrong done. The piano part
alone, with its powerful dotted rhythm, dissonant chords, and
voice-imitating triplets, proclaims it Brahms, and in its explosive
energy recalls the Variations on a Hungarian Theme op. 21, no.
2 composed about this time, and even foretells such later works
as the op. 79 Rhapsodies and the op. 118 Ballade. All six verses
are set, and if the quieter major middle section for verses 3, 4,
and 5 (the form is ABA) does not come up to the rest, it at least
brings a sense of variety and change of mood. The ballad ends
as it began, its postlude ringing out like a mailed fist battering
at the door for vengeance.

Like *Vor dem Fenster*, the fifth song, *Trennung*, is again about
lovers parting, but in complete contrast of mood. There is a
broad, tolerant humor in the folk poem that should appeal to
modern taste in such things. Far from yearning romantically outside the window of his inamorata, the lover is lying in delicious
but clearly implied illicit drowsiness in bed beside her after a
night of love. Like Juliet, she has to rouse her Romeo to awareness
of their perilous situation: the dawn is breaking, the watchman
is going his rounds, and the birds are beginning to sing. It is a
case of "Away, lad, before we're found out!" He hastily leaves her,
mounts his horse, and rides off, leaving her in regretful loneliness. The music matches the roguish mood of the poem in its
sense of breathless speed, its urgent 6/8 vocal line accentuated
by a superbly headlong accompaniment that unmistakably proclaims its composer. The pianist will revel in his share in the

song and, if he knows his Brahms, will be reminded of the similar but even greater challenge in the later Op. 28 duet *Der Jäger und sein Liebchen.*

The enchanting *Ständchen* closes the set. It is one of the loveliest of serenades, to be put along with those of Schubert, Strauss, and Brahms's own Op. 106, no. 1. Unlike the other serenades, the lover does not demand or even expect the girl to come out and join him. He only wishes her pleasant dreams in which he fondly hopes he will be a part. Only in the last verse does he suggest that the singing nightingale and shining moon wonder why he is in the garden and she in her room, separate and alone. Although the three longish verses are set strophically, the entrancing lilt of the melody allied with a beautifully rhythmic accompaniment full of beguiling modulations precludes any feeling of repetitiousness, particularly if both performers obey the composer's tempo and phrasing directions to the letter. The *allegretto* must be a real one, not an *andante,* and by the *leggiero* and slurred upbeats, faintly reminiscent of Schubert's *Hark! Hark! the Lark!,* the pianist must bring to bear all his artistry to convey the impression of a Viennese ländler.

We come finally to number 4 of the set, and I have left it to the last for a special reason, which is that although the text is thirteenth century, it is not anonymous, not folk, but a translation by Herder of a poem by Thibault (or Thibaut), Count of Champagne, who became King of Navarre in 1234. The poem, entitled *Ein Sonett,* is an impassioned avowal of love and adoration; and the difference between Brahms's setting of it and the others of the group lies in the fact that he treats it, not as an archaic text, but as though it were by Hölty or Daumer or any contemporary poet, with the result that the music is genuine contemporary Brahms, the warm-hearted lyrical composer of *Wie bist du, meine Königin* and others of the world's greatest love songs. The mood of the poem is caught and conveyed by a haunting, A$\flat$ melody harmonized simply in thirds and sixths, in ternary form with a falling plagal postlude of infinite tenderness, which expressed the old Minnelied character of the poem, and which (typical Brahms, this) unexpectedly in its last two bars changes from 3/4 to 4/4. Tenors should recognize it for what it is, namely, one of the most beautiful of love songs, and should make it known as such by including it in their repertories.

Although the *Five Lyrics for Solo Voice and Piano* of Op. 19 were not published until 1862, a year after the Op. 14 set, they are in fact coeval with them, being composed in the autumn of 1858, the later publication being in all probability due to the composer's inveterate habit of holding back works and reworking them until he was satisfied they did not fall below his own stringent standards. If this was the case, then they surely vindicate the delay, for here, more than in any previous set, they reflect the characteristics of the maturing Brahms, and this is in part due to the fact that the poems are no longer folk but of nineteenth or near-nineteenth-century German poets, thus demanding a "modern" interpretation in terms of music. This they indubitably received, for the voice of Brahms can be heard in every one of them.

With the first song, *Der Kuss*, we meet the earliest setting of Hölty, who was to provide the composer with texts for five further settings—all love songs and all masterpieces. The fact that the song was composed while he was at Göttingen and under the spell of Agathe Siebold explains at once why the passionate love poem appealed to him. "In the burgeoning May," says the poet, "I held her hand, looked into her eyes, and took her lips in a rapturous kiss. Like a consuming fire that kiss still burns through my whole being. When, O when will those lips let me know the peace that was mine before I tasted their sweetness?" Love was always a torment to Brahms. He yearned for it, but in the same breath he longed to be free from its shackles. His independence was everything to him, and there was always Clara in the background. More than the rest of his brief flames, Agathe was the one who came nearest to attaching Brahms to her, and so was made to suffer most of all. For as with Goethe and Lotte, to the mind of the genius so involved it was either escape or the death of the spirit. It is the fate of genius, in its colossal egoism, to cause torment not only to itself but to the women who come under its spell. This did not prevent Goethe and Brahms from immortalizing their passion. *Der Kuss* (like the G-major sextet) does just this. The lied is hauntingly beautiful in its slow, smooth rising and falling cantilena significantly marked *p molto expressivo*, which would-be performers must observe with the utmost scrupulousness. Its apparent effortless simplicity disguises two particular master-stokes: 1) it is almost entirely in 5–bar or

3–bar phrase-lengths and 2) the falling fifth of the unaccompanied bass in the 2–bar prelude forms the germ of the rhythm and harmony on which the whole song is built. The final touch of genius comes in the repeated "Kühlung zu!" of the coda following the repeat of the first strophe—a coda consisting of a mere four-and-a-half bars that yet, sung *p* above a now-richly harmonized version of the *ostinato*-like falling fifths, seems to express a world of infinite yearning.

The next two songs are companion pieces, deliberately intended as such, like the later *Regenlied/Nachklang* and *Sommerabend/Mondenschein*. Both texts are by Uhland, and both begin in the same key (D minor) and with the same melody. But whereas *Scheiden und Meiden* is an intense poem of only two quatrains in which the poet insists that there can be no thought of parting between lovers so lately in each other's arms and exchanging passionate kisses, *In der Ferne*, much longer, and by its very title more meditative and less impassioned, tells how the lover feels her loving thoughts of him through the singing birds, the stream, and the flowers that bloom alongside it. Brahms, therefore, while giving his settings a brief common premise, then proceeds to send them along totally different lines. The first, strophic and in volkslied style, with its eloquently mournful, 16-bar melody simply harmonized by upward-moving quavers in the bass line, perfectly conveys the suppressed passion of the poem. Its appeal lies in its very simplicity. For *In der Ferne*, Brahms, at the 12th bar, goes to major with delicious effect; but this is transcended by a Schubertian shimmer of color and sheer magic, when at "Will ruhen hier an des Baches Rand" he returns to the opening minor melody but keeps it major. The song ends with a note-for-note repetition of the first melody in the major ("Wie singet ihr"), but now given an accompaniment of quaver triplets suggestive of the lover's agitated questioning. As with so many other Brahms, songs one can only ask oneself sadly why these should be unknown, unhonored, and unsung.

That regretful query certainly cannot be asked about the next number of the set—*Der Schmied*. In fact, one is driven in all honesty to wonder whether it is more popular than its worth warrants. Brahms wrote literally scores of infinitely greater songs than this, which remain ignored and almost unknown while this and the *Wiegenlied* are familiar to everyone. Posterity has some unaccountable quirks to answer for. Be that as it may, one cannot deny that the square, folklike melody is immediately appealing (hence, partly, its popularity) and that the onomatopoeic accompaniment representing the blacksmith's hammer-blows on the anvil is a *tour de force*. Analysis or comment on so universally known a song would be superfluous. I therefore limit myself to throwing out a warning to the singer against taking Brahms's tempo indication, *allegro*, too literally. It is a misnomer. A jaunty *moderato* is quite fast enough: taken any quicker the vital weight of the melodic line becomes lost, to say nothing of the fact that the pianist will be made to sound like a tinker rather than the mighty blacksmith he is supposed to be.

No greater contrast among all Brahms's songs can be found than that between the previous number and the one that concludes Op. 19; and for that matter not only between those but between it and the rest of the thirty-one composed so far. With *An eine Äolsharfe*, we are confronted with a new Brahms and a lied that breaks completely new ground. There is nothing like it in Schubert or Schumann. Here is a Brahms whose feet have taken wings, who might never have associated himself with folk song or the strophic form and who, inspired by the ethereal quality of Mörike's poem, has transmuted it into even more ethereal music. The so-called "Harp of Aeolus," the supposed invention of St. Dunstan, has captured the imagination of poets and composers ever since James Thomson introduced it into his allegorical poem, *The Castle of Indolence* (1748), as an instrument of a lulling, runic character. Allusions to it are to be found in Berlioz, Cornelius, Reger, and Debussy, and Wolf was to give this same poem of Mörike's an equally beautiful setting thirty years later. The song is revolutionary for this early stage of Brahms's development, and remains unique for any stage of it. In many ways it anticipates Wolf and even Mahler. Gone are the established classical designs. The voice is given a rarefied freedom of line and tempo beyond anything yet attempted, and is allowed to catch every nuance of the poetic threnody. The song is a marvelously sustained arioso, part recitative, part aria. The dreamy harmonics of the harp are conveyed by the piano's *pp* chords placed high in the treble for the recitative and, for the arioso, above an *ostinato* of rising triplet crotchets. A final Brahms touch comes in the last fourteen bars (from the *poco più lento*) in which the rising and falling crotchet triplets in the left hand are set against four crotchets to the bar in the right. In the plasticity of its vocal line, its modulations, imaginative organization of the atmospheric accompaniment, and its overall sense of growth and unity, the song can only be described as a tone poem of haunting ethereality. Nor is it, as Ernest Newman in his Wolf fetishism asserts, put out of count by Wolf's setting. Both are masterpieces.

Summing up the songs Op. 3–Op. 19, one may state that, the few masterpieces duly noted apart, they reveal a composer who is steadily developing and striving to find his own individual voice and style. The intimations of higher flights and more mature works to come were soon to be fulfilled in the next set of songs published as Op. 32.

3

Deviation and Shadows

The next solo songs are the nine of Op. 32 and the fifteen comprising the *Romanzen aus L. Tiecks Magelone*, Op. 33, composed more or less contemporaneously. I propose to discuss the latter first.

It would be gratifying to the Brahms devotee to be able to point to the composer's only song cycle as being worthy of a place alongside those of Beethoven, Schubert, Schumann, and Fauré, but alas, this is not possible. To listen to or perform the work from beginning to end is an unrewarding task, leaving one with the impression that this is not the same composer who wrote the great songs we know.

Why? If we turn to dates and facts we shall be given clues. The first four of the songs were written as early as 1861, and numbers 5 and 6 the following year, the six being published in 1865. The rest of the cycle (nos. 7–15) took him five years (1863–68) and were published in 1869. So the fifteen songs took eight years to write. Clearly the work was a labor, but scarcely one of love. And the reason both for the time taken and the resultant mediocre achievement was, I suspect, that Brahms found Tieck's ultraromantaic oriental narrative of Count Peter's wanderings and adventures alien to his nature. The whole fabric is too long-spun, too excursive and flat, too like an opera libretto. While for this very reason it could have been an ideal incentive for, say, Weber, for Brahms, the least operatic of composers (the fact that he never attempted opera is significant) who needed the concentrated subjective lyric to bring the best out of him, the poems were too diffuse and the whole concept unreal and stagey. The cycle was probably conceived as a series of interlinked arias of a dramatic cantata somewhat along the lines of the large-scale Italian cantatas of Handel such as *Lucrezia, Apollo e Dafne,* and others. But whereas Handel's inborn dramatic genius enabled him to compose in a genuinely characteristic vein,.Brahms found the demands made on him by the story antagonistic to his very nature, and so could only produce music that, while always competent, is strangely neutral.

There is an analogy here with the verse plays of Byron, Shelley, and Tennyson, the operas of Haydn, and a good deal of the church music of Mozart and Schubert, in that the works tend to lack that special individuality of their creators' personal style. Similarly, these Magelone songs miss all sense of personal involvement. It is all very well to preach objectivity, but it has its limitations. Even in opera, the most objective of musical forms, the composer must convince us that he understands and feels for his characters before he can "put them across." In their song cycles, Beethoven, Schubert, Schumann, and Fauré make us feel that they are right inside the skins of their dramatis personae, and therefore we, too, feel for them. But here all empathy between composer and his hero and heroine is nonexistent: they are utterly colorless and become bores. The voice is not that of the real Brahms—only that of a ventriloquist manipulating puppets. In the corpus of Brahms's lieder, the cycle can only be regarded as a deviation from his true path, an experiment that failed.*

It is a relief to turn from the Magelone songs to those of Op. 32, where we are brought straight to the very heart of Brahms. It must be confessed that the heart so exposed is a melancholy one. This fact is so vital to any discussion of the lieder that some comment on it is essential. Biographical reasons have been found for the atmosphere of gloom that darkens so much of his work, especially over the period occupied by the rough drafts of the D-minor piano concerto and its coeval works. And because Brahms himself confessed to the personal reasons for the blackness of his spirit at that time, we must accept his confession. On the other hand, the truth is that external circumstances affect the

---

*It is not without significance that the one really great and characteristic song of the cycle and the one to be repeatedly singled out by anthologists should be the exquisite slumber song "Ruhe, Süssliebchen," that has nothing to do with the narrative as such.

creative artist surprisingly little. Temperament is the fundamental on which the superstructure of his creative imagination, moods, and emotions are built, and this, psychologists and psychiatrists tell us, springs primarily from the subconscious, which is unaffected by external events. People are by nature optimistic or pessimistic, lighthearted or serious, gay or gloomy. And it is the genius who is most seared by the curse of such temperament. Dante, Shakespeare, Swift, Johnson, Cowper, Gray, Byron, Musset, Chopin, Wolf, Housman, and Hardy are only a few of those who were notoriously prey to despair and pessimism, some to the point of hypochondriasis. Brahms can be added to the list. Many of his greatest works are, in Newman's words, "an emanation from the pensive melancholy that was the basis of his spiritual being."* Bearing this in mind, then, let us be wary of attaching too much personal significance to the fact that so many of the poems Brahms chose to set are pessimistic and disturbingly emotional. Some of the songs may well be an expression of his own emotions; equally they may be no more subjective than the more depressive lieder of Wolf or the more pensive *Mélodies* of Fauré.

Bearing this in mind, one cannot help being suspicious of the assertion, originated by Friedländer and repeated by later commentators, that "The juxtaposition of the nine poems contained in this work [viz. Op. 32] gives one a clear insight into the life of the composer himself. He tries to resist the spell of a beautiful and alluring woman, but finally succumbs completely."** In the first place, Friedländer does not cite the composer himself as authority for the supposition, nor do any of the others. In the second, the nine poems are taken not from one poet, as one would expect, but two—Platen and Daumer. Thirdly, if we examine the poems we are met with discrepancies and dubious premises. Thus the very first poem, for example, is not a love poem at all but a lament on the "squandering of time" when he, the poet, knows that life is so short and precious. The remainder, it is true, are love poems in different moods, some bitter, some grief-ridden, one defiant, another attempting to be jocosely cynical in the style of Heine. Only the last, the famous

*Newman, *More Essays from the World of Music.*

**Friedländer, *Brahms's Lieder* (London: Oxford University Press, 1928).

Wie bist du, meine Königin, expresses adoration and hope. Of course, like most theories, this of Friedländer's can be made to fit the facts, and cannot be disproved, so there may be a case for believing the set to be a revelation of Brahm's feelings for Clara or some other woman. Nevertheless, the analogy, I feel, is strained, and I prefer to regard the set as a series of separate, unlinked songs that simply transmute the poems and their different moods into equivalent music.

But let us put theories behind us and turn to the songs themselves. With this set of Op. 32 we are in a different world from the Magelone songs and most of the early ones. Here are no fumblings, no echoes of other composers—only mastery, strength, confidence, and originality generated by such splendid works that intervene between them and previous songs, as the vocal duets of Opp. 20 and 28, the "Handel" variations (Op. 24), the two piano quartets (Opp. 25 and 26), and the piano quintet (Op. 34)—all vintage Brahms.

The very first song—*Wie rafft' ich mich auf in der Nacht*— one of the greatest of the set, tells us that we are in the presence of the true successor to Schubert. For Schumann—though master of the miniature and indeed one of its greatest practitioners— was by no means Brahms's equal master in forms needing large-scale organization, and none of his songs can rival this one of Brahms's as a sheer, sustained, close-knit, through-composed organism. Brahms himself, in fact, in some ways never surpassed this song. Every shade and nuance of von Platen's poem is caught and magically transmogrified. The *pesante* bass octaves of the brief prelude not only provide rhythmic formula for the song but tell us that the composer's aural imagination has been awakened to the hollow sinister effect of unisons.

Ex. 11 *Wie rafft' ich mich auf in der Nacht*

This was to become a personal fingerprint. We shall find the same coloring in *Mit vierzig Jahren,*

Ex. 12 *Mit vierzig Jahren*

in *Feldeinsamkeit,*

Ex. 13 *Feldeinsamkeit*

in the second of the *Vier ernste Gesänge*,

Ex. 14 *Vier ernste Gesänge*

and in the *Intermezzo* for piano, op. 117, no. 3.

Ex. 15 *Intermezzo* for piano Op. 117

The shadow of the poet's sleepless nights and lost days (the theme of von Platen's poem) hangs darkly over the music, with its low, stark octaves and reiterated triplet quavers in constant cross-rhythm against the voice, emphasizing the despairing agitation of the poet. But at the picture of the night sky, with its moon and stars, the triplets rise in fourths and fifths into the higher register of the piano, taking over the generic rhythm above the vocal line and infusing the tonal darkness with a radiant clarity. The whole episode shimmers with light. But again the poet's thoughts become sombre at the contemplation of wasted time, to culminate in a cry from the depths of his being—"O wehe, wie hast du die Tage verbracht!"—magnificently captured by descending chromatic chords and timpani-like repetition of the doom-throbbing octaves by the piano, portraying a picture of mental desolation unsurpassed in music. In addition, the pianist is given a postlude of five magnificent bars of almost aching intensity, as though to disprove the criticism that Brahms, unlike Schumann and Wolf, lacked the imagination to provide fitting postludes to his songs.* For the equal of this masterpiece of close-knit yet expansive construction we must turn to the greatest songs of Schubert. *Wie rafft' ich mich auf in der Nacht* is for Brahms what the D-minor quartet, Op. 76 no.2 (the "Fifths") had been for Haydn—a historic landmark in their development in that after them neither quartet nor lied could be the same again.

If *Wie rafft'* is dark, the second song—*Nicht mehr zu dir zugehen*—is black, or, to quote Elizabeth Schumann, "almost neurasthenic."** The despairing lover, resolved never to have his wound reopened by sight or sound of his beloved, still cannot bring himself to the point of complete severance. "Give me happiness or utter forgetfulness" is the pith of the poem. Again we find the bleak octaves; but in place of the normal flowing vocal line the words are gasped out in fragmentary phrases as though the singer's emotions were too overpowering for controlled expression—a breathlessness reinforced by similar overlapping phrases in the accompaniment.

*See the Notes to the Brahms Song Society (1935). One is driven to wondering how these critics find substance for their comments. Do they imagine that the intrinsic worth of a postlude is in direct proportion to its length? Or consider the few bars that comprise almost all of Schubert's postludes to be "lacking in imagination"? As with Schubert's songs, those of Brahms in general do not call for long postludes: their very strength lies, often, in their terseness.

**See her *German Song* (1948).

Ex. 16 *Nicht mehr zu dir zu gehen*

The song is ternary, and the middle section, beginning with "Ich möchte nicht mehr leben," though more flowing, is filled with uneasy cross-rhythms and syncopations, and these lead into the *reprise* with its renewal of the pent-up, grief-laded phrases. The postlude continues the lead-footed, upward-climbing *motif* of the first bar of the song to a *f* climax, after which the lugubrious octaves sink into the lower regions of the piano as though into the abysses of gloom. In its originality and its technical and psychological achievement, it is comparable to the last Heine songs of Schubert.

Ich schleich umher, in contrast, is simple strophic, but none-theless profoundly felt. Platen's two verses are a lament express-ing the unreasoning unhappiness that can attack the heart of man. The reference to bare trees and faded flowers serves only as a backdrop to the poet's neurasthenic state of mind, and Brahms ignores it. The *angst* is conveyed by the melodic intensity of the vocal line, especially the chromaticism of bars 6–8 at "O frage mich nicht," and the rising phrases at "Das Herz erschüttert so manche Pein!," so expressive of anguish, emphasized by the bass, which, until now consisting of smooth, quiet downward-sliding sextuplet quavers, here breaks into agitated *forte* rising and falling triplets. Its very terseness and simplicity proclaim a master of song. Concentration is all. It is up to the singer, assisted by the all-important pianist, to give the melody the essential sombre color. So performed, no listener could fail to sense the song's tragic mood.

No greater contrast could be found than that between it and the next song—*Der Strom, der neben mir verrauschte*. Though the mood is yet again one of despair, here it is expressed by a highly organized through-composed song. "Where are the snows of yesteryear?" is the theme of Platen's poem: "where the stream, the bird-songs, the roses, the burning kisses your lips gave me? Where, above all, is the man who once was I? Where is he now?" Brahms's direction *agitato* is the keynote of the music's interpretation. The vocal line moves along in mournful rising and falling phrases driven on remorselessly by a formidable accompaniment of triplets with interjections of cross-rhythm rising octaves in imitation. Four times in the course of the song the time signature is changed from 4/4 to 3/2; and ten times the question *Wo ist?* is flung off by the singer in a frenzy of despair, the final *Wo ist er nun?* rising above a falling bass and a canonic echo in the treble in a cry of heartbreak, which the three-bar postlude in its murmured *diminuendo* seems to carry away into the far reaches of space. Like Haydn, but unlike Handel, Mozart, Verdi and the great operatic composers who could sustain drama over long span, Brahms could be intensely dramatic only in single movements or songs; and *Der Strom . . .* is just that.

The fifth song—*Wehe, so willst du mich wieder*—is the first of the set to escape from a world of grief and gloom. There is even a hint of defiant triumph in the poet's cry to nature to help him to break the bonds that are shackling him and to soar to realms where he can forget his grief. As such a poem leads us to expect, its musical interpretation races and soars. Marked *allegro*, it is the only quick song of the group. The two–bar *f* prelude with its powerful triplet quaver rhythm and ferocious chords of the ninth on the dominant might be taken for the beginning of a rhapsody for piano and prepares us for what is to come in this powerful, highly original song. However one examines it, whether harmonically, rhythmically, or melodically, it remains a staggering virtuoso piece. One of its astonishing harmonic features is that the tonic B minor is only briefly stated in the course of the song. The episode beginning with "Ströme der Seele Verlangen," with its excursion into flat keys and cross-rhythms, is particularly striking. Such is the headlong pace of the music and the harmonic and rhythmic variation within it that the listener is astonished to discover that the song is strophic! In contrast with the prelude, the imaginative seven-bar postlude, while beginning *f*, falls away in a lengthy *dim. e. riten.*, its penultimate bar slowing from triple to duple rhythm as though from exhaustion. Schubert's contemporaries, who complained that his songs were difficult both to perform and understand, would have considered this song of Brahms (and the previous ones of the set) to be impossible. Even today, adequate performance of it is far from easy and taxes singer and pianist to the utmost.

The text of the song that follows—*Du sprichst, dass ich mich täuschte*—has affinities with two poems of similar mood by the same poet (Platen), set magnificently by Schubert in *Die Liebe hat gelogen* and *Du liebst mich nicht*. The theme of all three poems is You once loved me, but confess now, you love me no longer. Schubert's settings are both intensely dramatic. This setting by Brahms, though sombre, is quieter and more ambivalent, begins in resignation, then passes to lacerating remembrance, and ends in a *crescendo* of grief that asks for release and forgetfulness. The prelude, with its thirds and sixths in the right hand above a bass of *ostinato* octaves, is one of the composer's most expressive.

Ex. 17 *Du sprichst, dass ich mich täuschte*

Note the little triplet figure in bars three and four: it will be encountered all through the accompaniment, now in the right hand, now in the left. Simple as it is it forms one more example of his subtle, all-pervading rhythmical sense. The second verse begins like the first, but after three bars it deviates, taking the voice higher and making it more transcendent for the inflaming "Dein schönes Auge bramte, die Küsse brannten sehr," showing that Brahms was far from being indifferent to a poem's inflections and nuances, as some critics have tried to make out. The accompaniment is varied, too, in a particularly skillful way in that the prelude is made to serve that purpose. The final verse is varied yet again both in the voice and the accompaniment, the bass of the latter now providing the rhythmic formula while the treble climbs in slow minims above it, after which, following a climax on high F for "und liebe," the voice falls slowly into its darker register as though overcome by remembrance. Under the slow "mich nicht mehr" of the voice's last phrase, the piano, now completely in the bass clef, brings the song to a close in a *crescendo* of anger and grief that ends unexpectedly in the major— a stroke of savage irony—repeating the basic 4–3–2 rhythm like a throbbing wound.

Judged purely as a "song without words," *Bitteres zu sagen denkst du* is one of the most melodiously beautiful in all Brahms; on the other hand it cannot be said to capture the mood of Daumer's poem, which is pretty inane anyway. The lover defies his sweetheart to hurt him with her bitter words since the lips from which those words come are so alluring that they are made sweet. Wolf himself, so susceptible to every nuance of a poem, might have been hard put to give this a convincing musical interpretation. Brahms makes it a love song purely and simply by setting it to a flowing expressive melody with a suave, equally-expressive accompaniment full of thirds, sixths, and diminished chords in the right hand above a left-hand rising figuration repeated through almost every bar of the song like an ostinato. In a major key (F), and, with the exception of a brief *forte* climax at "an korallner Klippe," marked *p dolce* throughout, the song is in sharp contrast to the preceding six songs, all turbulent and sombre and in minor keys.

The eighth song, *So stehn wir*, is the one comparatively ineffective and disappointing song of the set—a fact due, I am convinced, to the poem, which is so inapt in the context of the rest, so intransigent and discrepant, that one wonders why Brahms ever chose to set it. In a mood supposedly caustic and ironic, the poem, in feminine rhymes, declaims against the discord between "him" and "her," their altercations, and his inability to please her however much he tries. It is the sort of poem Wolf, in his most acid and detached vein, might have made musically convincing. But Brahms, though he could be humorous, could never be acid or detached, and was thus unable to make anything of it. Its flavor is so neutral, the vocal line so inexpressive, and the accompaniment so inert that neither the ear nor the mind is held by it.

To make amends, with the final number of the opus—*Wie bist du, meine Königin,*—we come to what I suppose may be regarded as the most popular and most frequently performed of all Brahms's songs. The reason for this favoritism is clear, namely, the sheer appeal of its melody, one of the most haunting in all music. Moreover, in it the overall mood of gloom of the preceding songs is broken. The lover finds consolation for his griefs in adoration of the loved one. "You are my queen, my adored, and emblem of all beauty. Death itself would have no fears for me if I could pass away in your arms." The melody breathes warmth and tenderness like a caress. But it is not just the melody that makes the song what it is. The accompaniment, though basically simple for Brahms, is full of subtleties that enrich it. We note the typical overlapping between voice and piano; the little interjections in which the piano either echoes or anticipates the melody, and its unobtrusive snatches of counter-melody; the overall construction as being a consummate example of the composer's varied strophic form; its perfectly proportioned symmetry; its catching of every nuance of the poem, especially by the darker harmonies and dissonances at the "Durch tote Wüsten wandle hin" in the third strophe with its reference to shadows and dessert wastes; and finally the inspired unexpected turn into the minor on "Todesqual die Brust" towards the end. Detailed comment or analysis is surely unnecessary: the song has sung itself into the world's heart as one of the greatest love songs.

Before leaving the song, and the set, however, I feel some comment is called for on the criticism thrown at it by, in general, anti–Brahms factions, who have made it almost notorious as a stick with which to beat him. I refer, of course, to the false stresses imposed on the very first line of Daumer's poem by the melody, which forces heavy and faulty accent on the syllables "wie," "meine," and "Königin." And a similar stone is found to throw at him in the later, almost equally famous *Die Mainacht,* where again the wonderful opening melodic phrase forces undue stress on the unimportant words "wann" and "durch." Such indifference to normal stress is undeniably a fault that would have made the more scrupulous Schumann and Wolf shudder. It shows, cries the anti–Brahms faction, that Brahms, having found his melody, looked for a poem that he could fit to it, instead of the reverse. The accusation is too silly to bother to refute. No song-writer of any worth whatever goes about setting poems in that way, let alone a master craftsman like Brahms. To anyone who knows anything about composition the melody of *Wie bist du, meine Königin* is purely and unarguably vocal to the point of being meaningless played on an instrument. Moreover, capturing the mood of the poem so perfectly as it does, it must have been inspired by that poem. While it is impossible for anyone, even a composer, to explain how a melody comes to him, it is my guess that after reading the poem and soaking himself in its atmosphere, the melody was given him by the first line of the last verse—"Lass mich vergehn in deinem Arm!"—which fits it perfectly, and whose mood of melancholy resignation could always draw the most deeply felt response from Brahms. He then found that his melody could not be made to fit the slightly different stresses of the first line. What was he to do—throw the whole song away? No doubt the problem must have caused him some anxious thought; but as it was a case of the whole song or nothing, he shrugged and let it go. It may well have been this song that caused him to assert that it was easier to write a through-composed song than to find a melody that would fit all the verses of a strophic one. Whether my supposition is correct or not, posterity can certainly be grateful that, false stresses or no, he allowed the melody to stand, and so endowed it with one more masterpiece. In any case, two further considerations can be added. First, such examples of carelessness in poetic stress are the exception rather than the rule (and the same applies to Schubert). Second, it is an elementary error to believe that a song that meticulously respects the stresses of a poem must of necessity be better than one that does not. The quality of the music is the prime essential, and a fine setting that captures the spirit and form of the poem but takes liberties here and there with accents is preferable to a dull one that respectfully hugs every syllable. If Brahms is occasionally insensitive to the natural accent of a word or the rhythm of a phrase, this is more than outweighed by his ability in that far-more-essential aspect, namely, the musical interpretation of the meaning of the poem. In this he succeeds no less than his great lieder compeers.

A final point. The song in question, along with many others, reveals that Brahms, being the great melodist he was, tended to think of the poems that he set in melodic rather than harmonic terms, being in this respect the opposite of Schumann and Wolf. To put it in another way: Schumann, who was primarily a pianist and had composed most of his best works for the piano prior to the upsurge of songwriting that followed his marriage to Clara, thought naturally from the piano upward, as did Wolf. His songs, in effect, are an extension of his pianistic thought. With Brahms the process worked in reverse. Most of his finest piano music (Opp. 76, 79, and 116–119 Klavierstücke) was written in the last years of his life and later than all his songs with the exception of the *Vier ernste Gesänge*, so that they may be said to be an extension of his songs, being indeed "songs without words" of beauty, intimacy, and forward-looking complexity unsurpassed by anything in the same field. This melodic bias does not mean, however, that his accompaniments are less harmonically interesting or less important than those of Schumann or Wolf, though he never allowed the piano to dominate as the latter did so often. He would never, for example, have brought himself, even if he could, to write a song like Hugo Wolf's *Und steht Ihr früh am Morgen auf**—a miraculous song in which the piano has all the "melodic jam" (as a singer friend once complained), leaving the voice to declaim through it. He would have considered it a waste of the voice and reversed the roles. To him the melodic line was the fundamental principle of song. From there, his marvelous contrapuntal, harmonic, and rhythmic skill took over to make the role of the piano an equal but not a more dominant partner. In their richness of harmonic texture yet unfailingly marvelous clarity so that they never mar the flow of melody but give added depth and character to the songs, his accompaniments are a perfect marriage between voice and piano, intertwining as closely yet independently as ivy round a tree. Even in his simplest Volkslied-like songs, as in his folk song arrangements, they have a characteristic life of their own, as *Sonntag*, *Ständchen* (Op. 14, no. 7), *Der Schmied*, or *Der Gang zum Liebchen* prove; and if any critic should rate them below his compeers, let him examine those of *Verzagen*, *Das Mädchen spricht*, *Auf dem Schiffe*, *Nachtigall*, *Auf dem Kirchhofe*, *Mit vierzig Jahren*, *Abenddämmerung*, or *Wie rafft' ich mich auf in her Nacht*, to name only a few. He

*Hugo Wolf, *Italienisches Liederbuch, No. 34.*

will find nothing more satisfying in Wolf or any other lieder composer.

With the exception of *So stehn wir*, this Op. 32 set consists of a series of infinitely varied master-songs, and singers considering doing some of Brahms could do worse than perform them as a group. It is a pity that Schumann was not granted another few years of life (he was only forty-six when he died) so that he could have known them and found in them the fulfillment of the prognostication he had made of the younger composer as "the eagle" and "he who is to come."*

*Karl Geiringer, *Brahms: His Life and Work* (London: Allen & Unwin, 1936).

4

Full Flood

From now on, with the exception of the three years separating Op. 84 and Op. 94, and the decade between Op. 107 and the ultimate Op. 121, there was no halt in the composer's outpouring of song. Compared with Schubert and Schumann, who in 1815 and 1840 wrote respectively 137 and 123 songs, his rate of composition may seem slow and his output meager. But Brahms was never given to fast and furious composition or to permitting publication of any work until his ultra-self-critical mind was satisfied that it was as good as he could make it.* In this, he was only carrying out his advice to George Henschel, the singer, apropos of a song he (Henschel) had written: "Let it rest, let it rest, and keep going back to it until is completed as a finished work of art, until there is not a note too many or too few, not a bar you can improve on."** The thirty-three songs composed mostly between 1864 (the year of his Op. 32) and 1868 contain many of his greatest. The latter year alone saw the publication of five song volumes: Four Songs (Op. 43), Four Songs (Op. 46), Five Songs (Op. 47), Seven Songs (Op. 48), and Five Songs (Op. 49). Nor did

---

*Brahms's habit of holding back works, sometimes for years, until he was satisfied with them, makes the actual date of composition of many of the songs uncertain and the year of publication nothing to go by. As an example, as much as a decade separates some of the songs of Op. 47 and Op. 48 (See Appendix, I). And, although the "8 Songs and Ballads" of Op. 57 were not published until 1871, Friedländer asserts, and I concur with him by reason of the common mood of so many of the songs, that they too were in all probability composed c. 1868.

**G. Henschel, *Personal Recollections of Johannes Brahms* (Boston, 1907).

this surge of lieder interfere with his output in other fields, for over the same period he produced the "Paganini" Variations, the piano quintet, the horn trio, the Deutches Requiem, the first cello sonata, the string sextet (Op. 36), the first string quartet, the Op. 39 Waltzer, and some of the Hungarian Dances, all in addition to the cantata *Rinaldo* and several part-songs. Brahms was at the height of his physical and mental powers, with creation in full flood.

Examination of the thirty-three songs covered by Op. 43–Op. 57 discloses the appearance of a new feature in Brahms—eroticism. This has nothing to do with the fact that a large proportion of his songs are love songs. In this he is no different from any song composer. Love—using the word in its widest sense—is after all the most common source of inspiration for both poetry and song. Brahms did not go in for exceptions, and the songs in question would call for no special comment but for the fact that some half a dozen of them are almost morbidly erotic. A cursory glance into his life may give us the key to this short-lived but violent incursion.

Schumann had died in 1856, and Clara, sensing that Brahms's respect and affection were on the way to becoming something more, left Düsseldorf with her large family the following year. She thus quietly withdrew from his life more and more. Nevertheless, she remained to the end one of the key influences of his life, and the separation affected him deeply. Then, human nature being what it is, in the summer of 1858 he met and fell in love with the soprano (all his more serious affairs were with singers) Agathe von Siebold. The mess he made of this affair and of her life is well-known. It is enough for our purpose to note that over the period during which the thirty-three songs in question were being written, he had been deprived or had deprived himself of the possible love of two of the women he thought more of than any others he was to know. It may not, then, be forcing biography to suggest that these circumstances may have driven Brahms, who after all was only in his thirties, to seek artistic outlet for his frustrated natural desires by setting poems that provided him with sensuous, if not downright sensual, images. This suggestion, I am aware, may seem to go back on my earlier remarks against the temptation to look for subjective biographical explanation in adverting to an artist's sources of inspiration. But if my words are examined carefully it will be seen that I was considering its application to a long-term, overall assessment of his work and I did not deny the temporary influences of some disturbing personal event. Furthermore, I am not asserting that the situation in which Brahms found himself at this stage affected his art as a whole. I bring in the biographical factor merely as a possible explanation for a phase that, though only temporary, comes strongly and strangely to the fore in these songs. Some of their very titles are suggestive: *Die Schale der Vergessenheit* (The Cup of Forgetfulness), *Liebesglut* (Love's Flames), *Sehnsucht* (Yearning), and *In meiner Nächte Sehnen* (In My Nights of Yearning). And Friedländer tells us that Brahms's friends were taken aback by "the hot passion and undisguised sensuality of many of the songs . . ." as well they might have been. There had been love songs before, but none so nakedly erotic as these, full as they are of references to lovers tormented by the fires of passion surging through their veins, by desire for their beloved's eyes and breasts and lips, and by vain sighs for the peace of forgetfulness.

Let us consider these songs briefly. The text of *Die Schale der Vergessenheit* (Op. 45, no. 3) is the most unrestrainedly erotic of them all. The poet (Hölty) cries out for a draught of Nepenthe that will bring him forgetfulness so that he will no longer be tormented by visions of his beloved with her "laughing lips, bright eyes, waving hair and heaving white breasts." Friedländer tells us naively:* "Brahms called the song worthless, and would not allow it to be printed." It appears that only the persistence of Julius Stockhausen, the singer and a friend of the composer, made the latter eventually give way. One suspects that the worth of the music had little to do with Brahms's misgivings about its reception by critics and public, and that its naked eroticism were more important to him.

With all respect to Friedländer, whose judgments are usually sound, I cannot agree with him that the song is an important one; nor is Brahms's assessment of it as worthless any nearer the mark. It is simply what might be described as competent but failing in what it attempts to do, namely, express unbridled eroticism. To be more explicit: at the passage in the poem, for example, where the lines speak of wish-forgetfulness and refer to Phaon and the Muse, Orpheus and Eurydice, and ask for a cup

*Friedländer, *Brahms's Lieder*.

from the Well of Sleep, far from attempting to convey the sense of languor and longing suggested by the words, the song, already marked *lebhaft*, breaks into a *poco animato* in which the voice sings a "square" sequence above a limping accompaniment and transmits no definable emotion whatsoever.

All the great songs of the world have one thing in common: they capture the mood of their poem. No one, even he did not know a word of German, could fail to sense that *Der Kuss; Ein Sonett;* and *Wie bist du, meine Königin* are warm tender love songs; that *Murrays Ermordung* is about something dramatic; that *An eine Äolsharfe, Abenddämmerung,* and *Lerchengesang* are nostalgic, and *O liebliche Wangen* joyous. And this is important, for if a song fails to interpret the poem's mood to the listener, mere technical competence counts for little. And this is where not only *Die Schale der Vergessenheit* falls down, but also *Liebesglut* (Op. 47, no. 2) and *In meiner Nächte Sehnen* (Op. 57, no. 5), with their "square" phrasing and rhythm. Musically competent, they cannot be dismissed as worthless, but they do not match up to the mood of their texts—and in that sense they fail. *Sehnsucht,* (Op. 49, no. 3) with its opening eloquent phrases, begins as though it were going to be a great song; but from the *lebhaft* onwards its quality deteriorates, in that the melodic line becomes more synthetic, the accompaniment conventional and empty (a rare occurrence with Brahms), and the song fritters away its pristine expectations.

But let us now turn attention to the three songs in which Brahms does succeed in re-creating on his own terms the aching passion expressed in the poems. These are all to be found in the Daumer settings of Op. 57 and are: *Von waldbekränzter Höke, Ach, wende diesen Blick,* and *Unbewegte laue Luft.*

The first is one of the most astonishing of the whole corpus of lieder that Brahms wrote. Indeed, one runs out of adjectives to describe it aptly: arresting, original, unique, baffling, and forward-looking spring to mind, but on their own seem insufficient. It is one of those works that at first hearing, or even second, one does not fully appreciate and tends to pass over as just lacking that divine spark that makes for indubitable greatness. There are many such among Schubert's lavish six hundred-odd songs— *Am Fenster, An den Tod, Dass sie hier gewesen, Tiefes Lied,* and *Florio* are just a few of them. Short of a golden age in musical appreciation, they will never become well-known or their true worth widely recognized. One has to dig and dig for their gold: and how many singers have the time or the will? Similarly with this song of Brahms's. Its pace is so fiery, its modulations so constant and wide-ranging as to seem at first even arbitrary, and the rhythmic flexibility so tensile that a first hearing simply cannot take in what it is all about and leaves an impression of a somewhat forced straining after originality. But if the listener or performer will only have patience and be prepared to go over it again and again and again until he has absorbed it, he will be rewarded by the discovery that as with so many things that are new and deviate from what are considered the typical and the usual, once the strangeness has worn off he will take it in his stride and be amazed, furthermore, at the gap between his first and his final impressions and opinion.

Let us first consider Daumer's very indifferent poem. This must have been one of the texts that so shocked Brahms's friends, for not only is it a passionate love message, but one from a girl who has the shameless audacity to declare her passion for her lover in no uncertain terms. Though separated from him, she sends him her kisses by the stream and the cloud, proclaims him her joy and despair, and concludes by saying that if only she could be with him she would bewitch him, and that her lips, her eyes, her bosom, her heart, and her soul are all his. No wonder Brahms's friends were taken aback!

And now let us see what the composer made of the poem. First to be considered is its formal organization, and this we find to be highly original and to consist of four linked episodes, each of fourteen bars. The first, after a 2–bar prelude that, marked p, is reminiscent, to those who have taken the trouble to make themselves familiar with the song, of a crouching tiger gathering itself for a spring. It begins in G major and closes at "zurück" in D major. A piano interlude leads into the second episode, which, beginning in D minor, closes in B major on a repeated "zu dir," with a downward swoop that will be used again in the home key for the voice's final close. Another piano interlude leads to the third verse, which ends in B minor, and from this a third piano interlude brings back a reprise of the first verse for eight bars, after which, through a coda that soars and swoops for the ecstatic "mit Busen, Herz, und Seele dein!," the song's eagle flight comes to rest. And throughout the song, the voice, carried almost recklessly along in a torrent of impetuous passion by a bravura piano part, plunges in and out first of distant flat keys then by enharmonic modulation into distant sharp keys.

Ex. 18 *Von waldbekränzter Höhe*

Is this merely license, we are tempted to ask ourselves, or inspiration at the highest level? First impression, I repeat, tends to make us lean to the former supposition. Only with closer study and growing familiarity do we begin to soar with the music and to see it for what it is, namely, not only one of the great love songs of the world but a finger-post pointing to Mahler and the next century. It is a pity that the high tessitura of the song (no transposition lower than a tone should be considered) and the sheer power and *élan* demanded by its climaxes, combined with the testing accompaniment when taken at the necessary speed (the *lebhaft* means here as fast as the pianist can take it), put it beyond the reach of all but the most accomplished professional recitalists.

The second of the three songs in question—*Ach, wende diesen Blick*—is in complete contrast. "Now, while my spirit is at peace, keep your eyes turned away from me, for one glance from them can revive the passion sleeping in my breast" forms the theme of the poem. Poems of suffering tinged with resignation in general suited Brahms's temperament more than those displaying a nakedly avowed passion, and this is no exception. By keeping the one slow tempo throughout, he marvelously catches the mood of resignation yet suppressed passion of the poem. The opening vocal line, entering without any prelude and accentuated by unisons with the piano, is eloquent.

Ex. 19 *Ach, wende diesen Blick*

At "Das Innre mir mit ewig neuer Glut," the lover's agitation is portrayed by triplets in the accompaniment that break in like ripples across a pool when a stone is thrown into it, while the voice rises progressively higher before falling back to the tonic F on "erfülle nicht!" In one bar, by the simple means of falling tones (A♭–G♭), a typically warm Brahmsian melody in D♭ unrolls in a perfect interpretation of the words, now expressing resignation and peace. But, matching the poem's ambivalence of mood, the return of suppressed passion takes the voice and accompaniment sequentially higher and higher, reaching climax on the high G over unexpected G-major harmonies, returning to the tonic F minor via yearning dominant sevenths. Friedländer perceptively describes this episode as "one of the deepest passages in Brahms's lyric works." From this point the song concludes with a *reprise* of the first section, making it ternary. But two small but important details need to be observed. Brahms gives the first bar of the *reprise* not to the voice but to the piano, holding back the former until the third beat on the word "Ein" and then not with the expected C but a D♭, making a momentary semi-tonal clash with the right hand of the piano. And finally, whereas the vocal line falls to its conclusion in a *diminuendo*, the two–bar postlude, recalling the fact that the poem's last line uses the image of a serpent that stings the heart, surges into a *crescendo* to end with a full *f* chord that rings out defiance, resentment, and foreboding.

Third, *Unbewegte laue Luft*. The poem, with its mixed, complex emotions and changes of mood, is a bristling challenge to a composer. Beginning as a peaceful nocturne describing a lovely summer twilight with a fountain playing softly in the garden and stars looking down, its mood changes abruptly as the poet contrasts this with the fever of love that runs in his veins, and his desire for the loved one who will not let him rest. But this mood, too, is evanescent, and the poem closes with an impassioned appeal to her to come out and share with him the mild peacefulness of the night. Clearly, only an onrunning song and a complex one at that could cope with the volatile moods of the poet, and Brahms creates just that. The opening 9/8 *langsam* is a superb piece of scene painting, languorous and as warm as the scene it depicts. The first change of mood at "Aber im Gemüte schwillt" brings a *lebhaft* in 4 meter, with agitated arpeggios in the accompaniment and impassioned rising phrases in the voice. But the most subtle touch is to come. At the poet's "Sollten nicht auch deine Brust," the opening *langsam* phrase of the song is repeated at the faster tempo, giving a wonderful overall sense of unity to the song. Finally, after an episode in F major (the key of the song is E major) by an F♮ = E♯ modulation the music makes a return to the home key at "Komm, o komm," with phrases reminiscent of the first bars of the *lebhaft* section, thus still further integrating the song. The final "Komm, o komm," now marked *p molto*, repeats the voice's opening phrase, and then with a *sempre dimin.* and *pp ritard e dimin.* the music, like the poem, dies rapturously away. The song is one of the most superbly organized, technically and emotionally, in all Brahms.

The six songs just discussed show that on rare occasions Brahms could let himself go, could give free rein to the bridled Romanticist within him, could lay bare the normally controlled passionate elements of his nature, and could still produce masterpieces. Let those who deny this take these songs to heart.*

The remaining twenty-six songs consist either of love songs pure and simple, often set to a background of natural beauty and in a mood of nostalgia, or of folk-settings.

If we consider the six volumes as a whole it has to be admitted that their quality is unequal. While including masterpieces, they also include not a few indifferent, uninteresting, and even uncharacteristic songs. Let us consider the latter first and then put them behind us.

The purposely archaic *Ich schell' mein Horn ins Jammertal* and *Vergangen ist mir Glück und Heil* cannot even be classed as lieder in the true meaning of the term, being deliberate throwbacks to a 16th-century modal style commensurate with the Old German text. Brahms must have realized that these *a capella*-style melodies and harmonies would be far more effective sung by a choir, for he arranged the first for male voices (Op. 41) and the second for mixed choir (Op. 62, no. 1). Even so, the innocent listeners, hearing solo or choral versions and ignorant of the substance of the texts, would almost certainly be under the impression they were listening to church music from the Palestrina era, whereas in fact the first is a very profane lament by a certain Duke Ulrich at being forced for political reasons to marry an unattractive woman and forsake a beautiful one, while the second is a lover's lament at being separated from his beloved one!

Das Lied vom Herrn von Falkenstein, a setting from Uhland's *Volksliedern*, and standing high among the candidates for being Brahms's dullest and least characteristic song, is a long-winded essay in the ballad style showing yet again (like the Magelone songs) his inability to make anything of a purely narrative poem. *Magyarisch*, a setting of Daumer, has nothing Hungarian about it, and its pleasant tranquil melody and smooth rocking accom-

---

*Among these must be counted Neville Cardus, who asserts dogmatically in his *Full Score*: "Brahms's expressions of passion were merely avuncular . . . with easily sentimental implications." One can only assume he did not know these songs.

paniment give us no idea of the smoldering passion of the poem. *Die Liebende schreibt* was composed a decade earlier than most of the songs comprised by these opus numbers. Goethe's sonnet had already been set by Schubert (Op. 165, no. 1) and Mendelssohn (Op. 86, no. 3). The former's setting can only be described as one of the worst of his mishits, his A major melody and easygoing accompaniment of triplets completely missing the pathos of the girl's letter and turning it into something like a hurried note to a man from his girlfriend saying that although she is having a good time she misses him all the same. The latter's setting on the other hand is not only one of his own greatest songs but one of the greats of all lieder and takes its place along with Vaughan Williams's *Silent Noon* and Britten's Michelangelo and Donne songs as being among the greatest settings of the sonnet form ever made. Brahms's version falls between the two, being neither as casual as Schubert's nor in the same class as Mendelssohn's. With its lightly moving 6/8 rhythm and, strangely for Brahms, unimaginative accompaniment, it simply skates over the depths of the poem. The other Goethe poem, *Trost in Tränen*, also composed in 1858, is no more successful. With its 6/8 meter and its strophic form with alternating major-minor episodes, it seems almost a deliberate copy of Schubert's even less-interesting interpretation. According to Friedländer, at least twenty composers have made settings of the poem. The fact that only those of Schubert and Brahms have survived at all and that even theirs are indifferent is partly explained, I think, by the poem itself, which, comprising four longish verses, has as its theme the not-very-inspiring assertion that tears are as necessary and sweet a part of life as joy. No doubt Goethe himself would have admired these settings for their simplicity and timid respect for his lines, and preferred them to such original masterpieces as *An Schwager Kronos, Erlkönig, Gretchen am Spinnrade,* and *Geheimes*. Wasn't his favorite composer Zelter?

The rest of the Op. 48 songs consist of folk-text settings, and even these, the well-known and charming *Der Gang zum Liebchen* excepted, with its Slavonic dance rhythm and Chopinesque *arpeggiando* accompaniment showing what Brahms in his maturity could make of a simple folk poem, are not to be counted among his best efforts in this line. The sad little F♯ minor *Der Überläufer*, in which the lover laments that his sweetheart has been taken from him by the "green-hatted huntsman," causing us to make comparison with the similar situation in *Die schöne Müllerin*, is the most appealing of the rest, neither the *Liebesklage des Mädchens* nor the *Gold überwiegt die Liebe* bearing the imprint of the master's stamp.

With *Am Sonntag Morgen* we come to infinitely greater things. The song, taken from the *Italienisches Liederbuch* of Paul Heyse, though short, is through-composed and subtly contrived, and matches the girl's mixed emotions. Her attempted indifference to her lover's falseness, masking her grief, is portrayed by a broken melodic line accentuated by a *staccato* and even more broken accompaniment, and her final confession of heartbreak culminates on the closing "die Hande wund zu ringen" by an impassioned climax for the voice above an accompaniment that in the right hand takes its own separate melodic way, and whose left hand consists of broken, upward-leaping triplets, dying away in an eloquent postlude that sinks lower and lower in a continual *diminuendo* into the gloomy depths of the bass register. The song, in its concentrated complexity, must be reckoned as being the nearest to the spirit and technique of Wolf, who would have recognized its originality in the sole fact that the accompaniment goes its own individual way and gives no hint of the melodie line. A song, in fact, not among those that instantly appeal, but one to savor, linger over, to study.

We are now left with fifteen songs, all of which should be in every lieder singer's repertoire, while at least half a dozen are to be counted as being among the heights of lieder. Coming to them in chronological opus numbering with the very first song of Op. 43, *Von ewiger Liebe*, we meet the ultimate Brahms. Even Wolf, blinded by his Wagner fetish and personal animosity to the point of being unable to see anything in Brahms, was moved to praising the song, despite one or two suspect accentuations. No doubt Brahms was particularly moved by the picture evoked in the poem. Two lovers are walking in the warm twilight. For some reason not explained in the poem, their love is open to public condemnation, and the lover, tormented and unhappy, wishes to know from the girl that she is not ashamed to acknowledge him before the world. If she has doubts, he says, then their love will be shattered as swiftly as it was formed. Iron and steel will rust and rot, she replies, but their love will outlive them and last for ever. The low, B-minor bass of the prelude, anticipating the voice's "Dunkel, wie dunkel," evokes the dusk and silence. Following the repetition of the eight-bar melody, as the lover voices his doubts and fears, the melody line rises, generating tension, and the accompaniment breaks into agitated triplets, becoming more impassioned as he finishes. The eleven-bar piano interlude, which follows his last words, is masterly, not only vividly conveying the lover's apprehensions, but with its *dimin. e ritard poco a poco* leads magically into the girl's reply in the major, quietly comforting at first, but rising to a first moderate climax— singers beware!—only to be repeated by a second and more powerful one, expressive of her resolve and the certainty of her love. No song even in Schubert is more spaciously conceived or designed than this nocturnal scene.

A final comment on the song. A few critics, while conceding it to be a masterpiece, have caviled at the syncopations introduced at the girl's climactic "unssere Liebe muss ewig bestehn!," maintaining that it is surely an error of judgment, at words declaring her unshakable love and faith, to make the music rock like a boat in a cross-current. I must confess to a grudging sympathy with the criticism, in that I believe that, as in a similar episode in the later *Auf dem See (II)* (see page 149), Brahms allowed the meaning of the words to slip into the background of his mind, and the instinctive instrumental composer, with his marvelous rhythmic subtlety, to take over where the more normal regular beat would have been more satisfactory. But even if it be admitted that the criticism is valid, it remains a minute detraction from a magnificent creation.

With the *Die Mainacht* of Hölty, a poet whose temperament was akin to that of Brahms, we keep to the heights. The poem contains all the ingredients that stimulated the composer's aural imagination: a nature scene combining with a dreamy introspection that throws a veil of pensive melancholy over what is superficially a picture of idyllic contentment. The nightingale sings, the moon shines, the doves coo in the coverts, but instead of reveling in the peace and beauty of the scene, the poet contrasts it with his own loneliness, and the sad thoughts engendered bring the hot tears to his cheeks. The scene is portrayed by one of Brahms's most glorious melodic curves underlaid by an accompaniment of dreamy, rocking quavers; but this, after the brief enharmonic section, suddenly erupts at the return of the tonic key into *f* chords and upward-surging triplets from the piano to be echoed by the voice in an outburst of despair on the words

"aber ich wende mich." A soaring and falling arch of melody at
"und die einsame Träne rinnt" brings this passage to a close in
the dominant, from which the original melody rises again, gain-
ing depth and intensity, only to die away in resigned grief. The
four-bar postlude, with its falling bass and rising treble, sings a
valediction of yearning and ineffable sadness.

It is a truism to say that the greatness of some songs can be
felt at once, whereas that of others becomes apparent only after
repeated hearing and study. This is why the more immediately
appealing works remain the most popular. The average con-
certgoer too often has neither the wish nor the will to look beneath the surface, and assesses on the strength of immediate
appreciation or non-appreciation. Thus, many of the world's
greatest masterpieces remain forever outside the popular repertoire. There are, for example, literally dozens of Schubert's songs
waiting to be discovered and sung by professional and amateur
singers alike. Similarly, Brahms has his more elusive songs, *Die
Kränze*, composed as early as 1864 though not published until
four years later, is one of these. The poem, by Daumer, is one of
those tear-laden messages to the beloved that were so dear to
nineteenth-century minor Romantic poets. The lover declares he
will hang the garlands, wet with his tears, over her door so that
when they "weep" over her she will know they are the tears
overflowing from his grief-stricken heart. Like Schubert, Brahms
was moved by these sentimental gushings into translating them
into masterpieces of song. The prelude alone is a stroke of genius. The whole song springs from it like a flower from a bud.
The *dolce*, D♭ harmonies capture the atmosphere of the poet's
sadness and resignation, while the rising and falling major sec-
onds form a repeated pattern that permeates it from beginning
to end.

Ex. 20 *Die Kränze*

The soaring phrase on the words "das Aug der Liebe," ending in one of Brahms's favorite gambits, a falling sixth, marks the first climax. After a slightly varied repeat of the prelude, an enharmonic modulation takes the music into C♯ minor, and this section, though given no change of dynamic, brings a sense of agitation by the accompaniment's pulsating quavers alternating with a renewal of the triplets. At "sei es auf ihres Hauptes goldne Pracht ergossen," while the voice drops chromatically in a spasm of grief, the piano, singing its monody of reiterated fourths above it, depicts the lover's falling tears.

Ex. 21 *Die Kränze*

The enharmonic return, five bars later, to the D♭ key signature, is a miracle that not even Schubert, the master modulator, surpassed, and it is achieved by the piano, which at the change of key signature, after echoing the previous phrase of the melody, falls a semitone, carrying the voice with it like a strangled sob.

Ex. 22 *Die Kränze*

The voice concludes with a repetition of the first climax; but
the nine-bar piano postlude, one of the longest and most expressive in all the songs, extends the emotional tension by the left
hand's alternating triple/duple rhythm and by the right hand
taking the prelude's rising melodic phrase in a swelling *crescendo* to an unexpected *f* climax a major fourth higher, repeating it immediately afterwards as if to accentuate the lover's
passionate grief. After this it fades away, still throbbing out the
first remoseless rhythm.

Ex. 23 *Die Kränze*

The song is an inspired amalgam of the Romantic and the Classical—Romantic in its emotional intensity, Classical in its control
and construction.

Yet, despite its being one of Brahms's most masterly creations,
no less than the more celebrated *Die Mainacht*, I can trace no

recording of it prior to that of Fischer-Dieskau, nor have I ever known it to be included in a recital.

The remaining love songs of this group stand in sharp contrast to those already discussed, and furnish proof of Brahms's wide emotional range. The well-known *Botschaft*, with its rippling, urgent accompaniment and lilting melody line, borders on hopefulness, and throws a ray of light into the overall gloom. Its mood and style have affinities with Schubert's *Liebesbotschaft*. Among its many felicities, one should note in particular the inspired extension of the melody in the second verse at "hochst bedenklich seine Lage," and the typical duple against triple rhythms, first in the piano alone, then taken up in the last verse by the voice against the piano and finally reverting to the piano to build a superb climax for the lover's "den du, Holde, denkst an ihn." A word of warning to the pianist here. It is no easy matter to give the accompaniment its requisite deftness, and accompanists tend to ignore the warning *p leggiero* given by the composer in the very first bar, with the result that the impression given is often that of a charge of heavy cavalry instead of the quiet murmured words of a hopeful lover.

Sonntag and *Wiegenlied*, both strophic, are among Brahms's most celebrated songs. The first, a setting of one of Uhland's *Volkslieder* (1844), miraculously catches the very spirit and form of folk song without sacrificing Brahmsian originality, proving the contention I made earlier that Brahms was so steeped in his native folk tradition that in some instances it is difficult to differentiate between his own and folk melodies. Along with *Der Gang zum Liebchen*, this song is a perfect example of that; and both are given depth by the addition of simple but highly original art-song accompaniments that are a joy to the pianist.

The second, also folk in its origins, must I suppose be in the running for a claim to be one of the most universally famous songs ever to be written. According to Friedländer, as far back as 1859 a certain Bertha Porubsky, with whom Brahms had had a mild flirtation, had made a deep impression on him with her singing, and one particular song by Alexander Baumann, typically Viennese in its Ländler rhythm, had especially stayed in his memory.

Du moanst wohl, du glabst wohl, die Lieb lasst si zwin - ga?

Ex. 24 *Wiegenlied*

Brahms simply transfers the rhythm of this melody to the accompaniment and gives the voice its own melody above it. Unsuspected by its thousands of admirers, this paragon of cradle songs, written in July of 1868 to celebrate the birth of a son to the singer (now Frau Faber), hides beneath its apparent simplicity a *tour de force* of technical achievement.

O liebliche Wangen, a joyous fast-moving love song, succeeds in combining passion with a half-playful jugglery with the poem's double rhymes—no small feat for a composer. It is also a superlative example of Brahms's genius for breaking the strophic form in order to give a fuller climax. In the first two verses the close is

Ex. 25 *O liebliche Wangen*

For the last verse, by the insertion of two bars, this becomes

Ex. 26 *O liebliche Wangen*

—a perfect illustration of Browning's "Oh, the little more and how much it is!"

The contrast between it and *Herbstgefühl*, probably composed at the same time, is overwhelming, but at the same time a perfect retort to any accusation that Brahms is more limited in his range than the other great lieder composers. No song surpasses *O liebliche Wangen* as a love song of exuberant elation; no song surpasses *Herbstgefühl*—except Brahms's own *Schwermut*, yet to come—as an outburst of passionate, unreasoning grief. The poem, by Schack, has close affinities with Collin's *Wehmut*, which had given Schubert one of his greatest songs, both lamenting the transitory span of human life, giving man so brief a time for the enjoyment of nature and its beauty. But whereas Collin's poem and Schubert's song are permeated with a resigned pensive melancholy, Schack's poem and Brahms's song exude a searing pessimism. The depressing feelings engendered by autumn, with its nipping winds foretelling winter, its falling leaves, gray skies, and first frosts, are vividly expressed by the mournful *pp sempre* F♯-minor descending thirds of the prelude and a sense of numb desolation in the static vocal line.

Ex. 27 *O liebliche Wangen*

At "so schauert über mein Leben," the music breaks into a contrasting *f* of desperation expressed by long, urgent chromatic phrases for the voice and *agitato* triplets above hollow descending octaves in the piano. Then this fades in a long *diminuendo* as though the singer were exhausted by the emotional outburst, and the song ends with the same numb grief with which it began. Not even the most tragic songs of *Winterreise* go beyond this masterpiece for sheer starkness.

An die Nachtigall and *An ein Veilchen* tend to be linked in the mind as being closely related. Both were composed in the summer of 1868, both are songs of love-longing with a background of nature and beauty, both are in the same key and both texts are by the same poet—Hölty. Schubert had set the former in 1815, giving it a strophic form and a pensive melody in the minor (F♯). This masterly setting of Brahms, however, has put it out of court: there is simply no comparison to be made. To begin with, Brahms's melody is of the purest and most haunting quality, sung over a rocking syncopated accompaniment suggestive of the sighs of the listener as, standing in the dusk among the apple blossom, he hears the nightingale pouring out its heart in love to its mate. The piano's linkage between the second and third strophes—to be repeated almost note for note in the as-yet unconceived *Sapphische Ode* of 1844—leads to what looks as if it were going to be a repeat of the first verse, but instead proves to be a perfect example of that unique variation sense of Brahms's on which I discoursed earlier. After a *f* climax (the only one) on "dem Himmel an," the syncopations in the piano lead us back to the melody of the second strophe, but now the accompaniment has its own variation, for not only does it break into softly-falling triplets against the voice's 4/4 pulse, but it sings its own harmonized countermelody, which towards the close of the song sinks in a gradual *diminuendo* to fade away as ethereally as the song of the nightingale itself.

In discussing its almost twin, *An ein Veilchen*, it is difficult not to repeat much of what has already been said. The poem has a similarly sentimental theme to the *Die Kränze* of Daumer from which Brahms fashioned a masterpiece, and he was to repeat the process here with Hölty's equally tearful outpouring in which he wishes that the dew on the flower shall be seen by his beloved as the tears of longing and grief he is shedding for her—longing to the point of death. Again we have a melody of incomparable beauty, this time in 6/8, with one of Brahms's most original accompaniments. It would have been so easy for him to have harmonized the melody line by means of simple quavers, as we so often find in Schubert. Instead we are given:

Ex. 28 *An ein Veilchen*

along with, later, little interludes from the piano that echo the voice like sighs. The music modulates gloriously, passing from the tonic E major through a series of colorful modulations, only to plunge unexpectedly back into the home key via the piano in preparation for the "O dann schmiege" of the middle verse. Here the accompaniment is given a different, more *agitato* figuration, while the voice, with an off-beat pulse, climbs up via a long *crescendo*, taking alternating 9/8 and 6/8 bars in its stride, to its one *f* climax on "dich ihr ans Herz." After this, following a three-bar subsiding interlude from the piano, the first melody returns for the last verse to merge into an eloquent coda. The word "Tod," like "Liebe," never failed to strike a strong chord in Brahms, and thus to give him inspirational touches. So it is here: the phrase "und den Tod wünscht" (with "den Tod" repeated), echoing the earlier modulations, veers magically in five bars through C, F, and E, with the voice dying away on Brahms's most-favored close—the falling sixth. The seven-bar postlude murmurs the opening phrase of the song before fading out in a dying fall.

Both songs are supreme examples of that simultaneous harmonic richness and clarity about which I spoke earlier.

Like so many of Brahms's greatest songs, *Abenddämmerung*, the last of Op. 49, is permeated with nostalgia. With the shadows of twilight, says the poet (Schack), come memories of childhood's days and of friends lost by circumstance or death. The accompaniment, from the seven-bar prelude, one of the longest and most impressive of them all, is one of the greatest achievements in all lieder. Marked *ruhig* and *dolce p*, the inspired figuration and *motif* of the prelude, with its rising and falling line, prismatic harmonies, rocking rhythm, and a pedal bass interwoven with a cellolike countermelody, run through almost the entire song, knitting it into a miraculously unified whole.

Ex. 29 *Abenddämmerung*

Only for the A-major episode at the verse, in which the poet, envisaging himself sitting alone in the firelight, conjuring up recollections of his childhood home and friends so vividly as almost to feel their presences, does the music throw off its *osti-nato* figurations. And here Brahms, in a moment of sheer inspiration, modulates to the subdominant, and, in a passage in which the accompaniment is filled with false accents, harmonic uncertainty, and vaguely suggested imitations of the voice, marvelously transforms the nostalgic mood and flickering shadows of the poem into an even-finer musical picture. The whole passage is worth quoting.

Ex. 30 *Abenddämmerung*

Following this, a return to the original key and figuration is made by a wonderfully conceived four-bar modulation, and the song is rounded off by an aesthetically satisfying repetition of the first strophe, the voice ending with the composer's favorite falling sixth, the piano being given an inspirational three-bar postlude in which the pedal bass, the tenor countermelody and the rustling right-hand semiquavers, falling and rising, die away to silence on the long-held tonic chord. The song is assuredly one of the composer's greatest songs.*

We thus arrive at the eight songs of Op. 57. These are in the main a gloomy lot, though, beginning and ending with the two masterworks I have already described, *Von waldbekränzter Höhe* and *Unbewegte laue Luft*, which lighten the overall gloom, the former with its uninhibited joyous passion, the latter crowning the series with an appeal for understanding, harmony and peace.

With one exception, the others are sad enough. *Wenn du nur zuweilen lächelst* and *Strahlt zuweilen*—numbers 2 and 6—have affinities in that both are more restrained, more lyrical than the rest, and in a sense are at one and the same time the complement and antithesis of each other. In the former, the poet, hungering for some sign of sympathy from his beloved, begs merely for a smile to lighten the gloom of his unhappiness and to help him to bear her coldness with patience and hope; the latter becomes a palinode in that, having now been granted his request, he tells her that those same smiles that first won his heart, while friendly, pierce him like daggers because they are friendly and nothing more, and fall short of the love he craves. *Wenn du nur* is perfect in its lyrical tenderness and expression of sad resignation. The lilting 9/8 melody sung above warm, E♭ harmonies,, gently flowing yet broken by interrupted phrases, movingly conveys the longing of the appealing lover, which, rising as though it were beyond his control, soars to its climax at "Alles treiben lassen, was der Liebe wehe tut." On the final "wehe tut" the C♭ pierces the heart like a strangled sob. The five-bar postlude is masterly. Beginning as though it were going merely to repeat the first bars of the accompaniment (which has no prelude), it proceeds to jump the second bar and link with the third, which again is altered in its second half so as to echo the poignant C♭ of the

*Yet how often does one hear a performance of it? And apart from Fischer-Dieskau's recording, there has been only one other.

voice's "wehe," in turn to be echoed as C$\sharp$, from which it falls tone by tone to the final E$\flat$ chord like a renunciatory sigh. The song repays endless study as a magnificent example of profound effects achieved as effortlessly as anything in Schubert.

With *Strahlt zuweilen*, a different note is struck from the despairing pleas of the other songs. The music is lighter and still more lyrical in its 6/8 rhythm; and though the ear welcomes the relief, it has to be admitted that it does not quite match the smothered pangs of the lover as expressed in the poem, especially its last two lines. As against this, it is a beautiful example of Brahms's masterly handling of the varied strophic form, with its lovely Schubertian major-minor alternating modulations, and melodic and harmonic variation for the second verse.

Es träumte mir is a masterly evocation of a mood. "I dreamed you loved me. But even as I dreamed I knew it was a dream," is really all the six-line poem amounts to. The song has affinities with the more poignant examples in Schumann's *Dichterliebe* in its overall style and sentiment. Brahms achieves a dreamlike aura by a sequence of pp arpeggios in the left hand (suggestive of dreams permeated by rising tides of consciousness) that persist like a *leitmotif* from the first bar to the last, and by isolated static chords in the right hand, above which the voice floats in a slow 6/8 rhythm like a disembodied intonation. The moving postlude dies away to nothingness, seeming to vanish along illimitable vistas of dreamland. Only a consummate artist can hope to do justice to this consummate song.

Doubtless, *Die Schnur, die Perl' an Perle*, the setting of a poem that expresses desire to be in the place of the brilliant necklace that, wrapped round her throat, "lies, pearl on pearl, along her lovely bosom," was regarded by Brahms's friends as one of the more erotic and less "nice" songs. But really it is no more than a German version of Tennyson's equally inane 'The Miller's Daughter':

> And I would be the necklace,
> And all day long to fall and rise
> Upon her balmy bosom
> With her laughter and her sighs,
> And I would be so light, so light
> I scarce should be unclasped at night.

Looking back on such poems from this day and age, the only reaction is wonderment that poets could be so naive as to write such stuff and readers so gullible as to swallow it. But that was the nineteenth-century way of cultivating erotic safety valves: and if the Victorian Tennyson could get away with it, why not the German Daumer? The latter does at least put some body into his effusion by declaring that his love would be crowned if his heart were only allowed to come to rest "on a place so fair." In his musical interpretation of the poem, Brahms gives us, if not the poet's "white-hot flame of rapture," a song that in its lilting, haunting melody, modulations, and onrunning semiquaver accompaniment, glows with passionate tenderness. Through-composed, the music becomes a kaleidoscope of similar but ever-changing patterns modified with infinite resource and variety; the whole song being, in fact, a rare example of that continuity, the "art of imperceptible transition," of the snake making a fulcrum of its own body in order to progress,"* of which I spoke earlier. Unusually, the song has no postlude, but the closing bars, in which the voice broods on repeated F♯s while the piano takes over the melody, do good service for one. The long suspension on the final "Brust" comes like an ardent sigh.

With the songs of Op. 57, we leave Daumer and his sultry love verses. After them, Brahms was to set only three more of his poems. In all he made nineteen settings of his most-favored, if mediocre, poet, of which thirteen are among his greatest. Let us not cavil, therefore, at his want of literary taste. By these songs he gave Daumer's name a celebrity his poetry could never have achieved for him in his own right.

This collaboration between poet and composer gave rise to an amusing episode. In the May of 1872, feeling he must thank the poet for the inspiration he had given him, Brahms broke a journey in order to call on him at his home in Würzburg. He found a shriveled old man who knew nothing of the composer or his songs. When Brahms enquired jokingly about the lovers and love affairs described so passionately by the poet, Daumer, chuckling, went into the next room and brought back a little woman as old, tiny, and shriveled as himself, and presented her to Brahms as

---

*Ernest Newman, "Brahms and the Serpent."

"the only woman I have ever loved—my wife."* The moral of this—never believe poets—may well have struck Brahms very forcibly.

*Max Kalbeck, *Johannes Brahms* (Berlin: Deutsche Brahms Gesellschaft, 1904–14).

5

Mastery

Not surprisingly, by 1868 Brahms was making a reputation for himself both as a song composer and pianist—so much so that in the spring of that year he went on a concert tour with Julius Stockhausen. The composer and the singer had first met at the Rhine Music Festival, Düsseldorf, in 1856, and ever since, the latter had been not only one of his staunchest friends but an admirer and interpreter of his songs. In his *Brahms: His Life and Work*, Karl Geiringer writes: "Many of Brahms's finest songs were written expressly for Stockhausen, and he was the first to introduce them to the concert hall."* To have heard Stockhausen singing the songs actually accompanied by the composer must have been for their audiences much as the performances of Vogl and Schubert had been for a previous generation and as those of Bernac and Poulenc, and Pears and Britten for ours. (Note: it is usually the pianist who is the composer). It may not then be farfetched to believe that, with such an interpreter of his songs at hand, and encouraged by their successful tour, Brahms should, for the time being at least, have been led to concentrate more on writing songs than instrumental works.

Be that as it may, the fact remains that between 1868 and 1871, while publishing four volumes of songs in addition to the *Liebeslieder Waltzer*, the *Alto Rhapsody*, *Triumphlied*, and *Schicksalslied*, the only instrumental works to be put on paper over the same period were the C-minor string quartet (not completed until 1873) and possibly a few of the Hungarian Dances. Clearly

*Geiringer, *Brahms: His Life and Work*.

at this time the vocal field held foremost place in his musical consciousness.

The first of the new songs to be published were *Songs and Melodies,* Op. 58. Freed from the sultry passion of Daumer, the songs have a different emotional climate from the previous set. None of the eight can be described as erotic; and though three of them are steeped in despair, four are positively shafted through with rays of hopeful love. The first, *Blinde Kuh* (Blind Man's Buff), is a *tour de force.* The lover, groping about in the dark trying to find his sweetheart, complains that he is lost, and pleads with her to come from her hiding place. The first two verses are set strophically, and the G-minor melody has a folk-song-like quality borne along by the piano's helter-skelter semi-quavers. The third verse goes major and *più animato,* and ends with the voice, now frantic with appeal, in successive leaps of a third, a fifth, and a seventh, after which both hands rush up the keyboard in arpeggios. The accompaniment, in fact, is from beginning to end a *moto perpetuo* of whirling semiquavers and a challenge for any pianist. The text, a translation from the Italian by Kopisch, is presumably meant to be taken allegorically, like the later *Nachtwandler.*

Während des Regens is the second* of Brahms's four "rain songs," and the only one where the rain is not seen as the emblem of tears, that is to say, is not tragic. Quite the contrary, in fact. The girl asks her sweetheart to kiss her as long as the rain falls, and to stop when it stops, at which the lover, naturally, implores the rain never to leave off. The broad, sweeping melody rises and falls above the fast, pattering quavers in restless modulations and alternating 6/4 and 9/4 meters. It is an attractive, exhilarating song and one that should figure far more prominently in recitals.

Equally relaxed and enchanting is *O komme, holde Sommernacht.* Far from being the more usual somber night-piece, the poem is a welcome to the summer evening, greeting it all the more rapturously because the poet knows the girl returns his love. Brahms chooses the bright, ringing key of F♯ to express the lover's exuberance, with the piano rippling in dancing quaver

---

*The first was the *Regenlied,* of uncertain date (1862–66). That Brahms was dissatisfied with this rather colorless song is shown by two facts (1) he did not allow it to be printed in his lifetime and (2) he made another setting of the poem as *Nachklang*—the one instance in all his songs of two settings of the same poem.

triplets, now in the right hand and now in the left, persisting from the first bar to the last, the voice meanwhile giving out a melody full of leaps indicative of confidence and delight. And yet (warning to singer and pianist) the dynamic never rises above p. Indeed, Brahms carefully stresses *molto p, leggiero, mezza voce,* and *PP sotto voce* successively in the piano part; and the voice's closing phrase, so triumphant, so tempting for a singer to "let go," is specifically marked p. What the composer had in mind is the picture of a lover so rapt in his happiness that as he walks he murmurs the words half to himself, half to the summer-scented air, like a secret. And in the postlude's diminuendo to pp we can almost visualize him disappearing in the hazy distance, walking on air. The song is a little masterpiece redolent of young love, spring, stars, flowers, and dreams.

No greater contrast could be found than that between this song and the next: *Schwermut.* One mentally associates it with that other tragic cry, *Herbstgefühl* (Op. 48, no. 7). If that is autumn, this is winter; if that is dark, this is black. In five devastating lines, the poet (Candidus) simply yearns for "the eternal night" that obliterates all sentience. And since Brahms's innate pessimism made him in darker moments familiar with this mood of life-weariness, he was able to match the black soul of the poet with his own. The tempo indication *sehr langsam,* the dynamic *sotto voce,* and the key of E♭ minor tells us in advance the kind of song we are to expect. The slow, repeated minims of the prelude make the aura of despair almost visual, and the voice's initial phrase, "Mir ist so weh ums Herz," is a desolating cry of naked grief. At "mir ist, als ob ich weinen möchte," the voice rises slowly, heavily, from A♭ to E♭ in a gradual *crescendo,* attains f on the high F at "vor," then falls through a fifth to B♭ as though drained by the effort.

Ex. 31 *Schwermut*

Only with the change of time-signature to 4/2 at "Möcht ich das Haupt" is there any relief from the block-hewn static harmony, and here the piano's slow rising arpeggios bring a grudging sense of movement as though desperately trying to throw off the shadows and emerge from the all-pervading gloom. But the voice, oblivious, continues its mournful monody, and in the postlude these same arpeggios, as though giving up all hope, sink lower and lower, become fainter, until they die altogether in the final, long-held, disembodied semibreve major chord. This is complete annihilation; a negation of life itself. Never before, not even in the bleakest songs of *Winterreise*, not even in that interlude of sheer heartbreak that comes between the slow movement and the finale of Mozart's G-minor string quintet, had human hopelessness been so searingly expressed.

As against the three high achievements just described, we now have to admit to three less successful ones: *Die Spröde, In der Gasse,* and *Vorüber.* The text of the first, another Kopisch translation, might qualify for classification as uncomposable, though again, as with the Op. 32 *So stehn wir*, Wolf could perhaps have made something from it. But a poem of three verses that declares in the first that the poet has moved a tigress to pity by his sighs, in the second that he has dissolved a granite boulder with his tears, and in the third, as against this, he cannot bring his sweetheart so much as to pity his plight, does not seem to give much scope to a composer. Brahms gives it one of his varied strophic settings. The trouble here, though, is that the somewhat jaunty, rather commonplace, melody of the first two verses does not cohere with the pathos of the last verse, attempted by means of major-minor alternations and restless interchanging 3/4 and 2/4 bar lengths, and altogether leaves little impression on the mind.

In der Gasse has similar defects, made to appear even worse in that its theme immediately compels reference to Schubert's *Der Doppelgänger*, one of his greatest songs. The scene portrayed is identical—the empty street, the now-deserted house, the mocking moonlight, the lost love. Brahms's second strophe is impassioned enough, but the first merely skims the surface with once again a lack of unity and unequal inspiration. With *Vorüber*, it is the reverse. The poem opens with a scene of nocturnal beauty and nostalgia— two things that always drew the best out of Brahms as songs such as *Die Mainacht, Sommerabend (II),** *In Waldeseinsamkeit, An die Nachtigall,* and others testify. The first section of this song is no exception, the poem's atmosphere being magically captured by a languorous melody made even more expressive by one of the composer's most free and most arresting basses that is an inspiration in itself. Note (1) how he skillfully places the melody in the most expressive *tessitura* of the voice, and (2) how the three-bar opening phrase of the vocal line has its echo in the piano to complete it and turn it into a four-bar phrase—a Brahms fingerprint.

*I have added the numeral in order to distinguish between it and *Sommerabend* of Op. 84.

Ex. 32 *Vorüber*

Had the song continued at this level, it would have taken its place with the outstanding songs mentioned above. That it fails in this is due to the weaker second half, which, with the poem's sudden change of mood from the "Denn nun ich erwache" onward, its reference to "withered leaves," and its death-yearnings, becomes hectic rather than profound; and the song, split as it were into a dual personality, falls off in quality like several others of the composer's longer lieder.

The set is rounded off by the charming if somewhat conventional *Serenade* (Schack), complete with the inevitable guitar accompaniment, plashing fountain, Italianate thirds and sixths, moonlight, shady trees, and lover's plaintive sighs. Though it does not match the famous Serenades of Schubert, Strauss, or Brahms's own Op. 106, no. 1, I recommend it to singers as something different from the general conception of Brahms, and as providing an attractive number in a group of his more typical lieder.

With the *8 Lieder und Gesänge* of Op. 59 and the *9 Lieder und Gesänge* of Op. 63 we are taken into the early 70s; and from now on the unsatisfactory lieder become few and far between, and memorable songs the rule rather than the exception. There is as yet no change in style—the terseness and concentration of the later songs lie ahead—but now Brahms has made himself master of his material, his lyricism becomes even deeper, and the forms in which it is cast become more and more mutable. In the instrumental field, this new richness can be seen *in excelsis* in the only nonvocal works composed at this period: the A-minor string quartet and the "Haydn" Variations.

The Opus 59 set opens with *Dämmrung senkte sich von oben*, a setting of Goethe. Goethe—great poetry at last. What will Brahms make of it? one asks in anticipation. His two previous settings had been disappointing; but here, surely, opportunity is at hand, for the poem of the great poet, written in his old age, gives the composer all the ingredients he looked for: a nocturnal setting; pensive meditation; descriptive pictures—twilight vaguely lighted by the rising moon, willows casting their shadows over the lake—and concluding, not as so many of such poems do, in nostalgia or despair, but in complete tranquility of spirit. All passion spent is the meaningful core of the poem. Yet, perhaps for the very reason that it did not express nostalgia or grief, Brahms failed to capture its essential atmosphere. The music is heavy and oppressive rather than tranquil, and misses the radiant serenity of Goethe's lines; and this pervading sombreness is emphasised by what can only be censured as the misplaced *tessitura* of the voice almost throughout, which is more bass than baritone. This is particularly felt in the last five bars, at the repeated "sänftigend ins Herz hinein," where Brahms, just where the poem clinches all that has gone before, takes the voice lower and lower to end on low G, thus underlining the darkness of the scene instead of the light. The fact that he gave the singer an alternative version that rises instead of falls and is much to be preferred, shows that he must have had doubts as to the fitness of his original thought. An incidental point of interest is provided by bars 13–16 of the vocal line, and the repetition in the first four bars of the major section. Listening to the song, the Brahms-lover must be startled into asking himself why the melody is familiar to him. The answer is: the last movement of the second clarinet sonata written two decades later. The throwback resemblance is a clear case of that subconscious remembrance and repetition of earlier works that haunts so many composers.

Coming next to a minor poet, typically Brahms is inspired to bestow immortality on him. Simrock's *Auf dem See* is an idyllic nature scene full of color, and breathing peace and beauty. All the composer's heart and mind leaped to meet the picture provided by the poet—a picture not only beautiful in itself but tinged with philosophical implications of man's place in nature. The combination of the two drew from the composer a masterpiece that without exaggeration may be regarded as the quintessence of his lyrical genius. The bewitching melody rises and falls in smooth curves suggestive of the rocking boat over an accompaniment that is a barcarolle in itself. The first two verses are treated strophically, but for the third verse, following the nuance of the lines that refer to "Stürmend Herz, tu auf die Augen," the accompaniment with its rising triplets becomes more agitated, and the melody line more extended and upward-reaching, imparting deeper issues and more pensive thoughts. But this soon subsides, and the last verse is a repetition of the first two. The song is a sheer delight to singer, pianist, and listener alike; and in the lines "Also spiegle du in Liedern/Was die Erde schönstes hat" every Brahms lover will read the composer's epitaph.

The level of inspiration obtains over the ensuing two poems of Groth, which are companion pieces in that they have a common basis of inspiration, namely, the rain, which brings nostalgic memories to the poet of childhood days. Brahms links the two by using the same melody and accompaniment initially for both, though his treatment of them varies. If the *Regenlied* is somewhat less successful than the *Nachklang*, that is because the poem is longer (with thirty-six lines) and more diffuse, making it more difficult for a lyrical composer like Brahms to unify. And indeed the strain is felt, if only slightly, in the smoother D-major section, which does not quite come up to the rest of the song. The second poem is not only much shorter (a mere nine lines) and therefore more concentrated, but is at the same time expressive of a much sadder mood. Whereas in the first, the poet simply stands back, as it were, and after recounting the happy scenes of his childhood in gentle nostalgia, wishes he could recapture the magic of those days, in the second the rain is echoed by his bitter tears of grief as he reflects how different his life is now and on what might have been. This gave Brahms all he needed to produce a song that doubles the concentrated intensity of the poem—a song that is heartrending in its melancholy perfection. The rain and the poet's tears are portrayed in the right hand semiquavers of the piano, the nostalgic grief in the reiterated ♩♪♩ rhythm, now in the bass, now in the treble, which permeates the song, and in the mournful minor phrases of the melodic line.

Ex. 33 *Regenlied*

Although the song closes in the major, the postlude brings no feeling of relief. Rather, by its continuation of the deliberately monotonous pattering quavers and its initial rhythm remorselessly pursued in the higher region of the piano, its urgent *crescendo* and *f* climax followed by a *diminuendo* ending in three quiet major chords, the sadness is intensified. It is a haunting piece of music, and one can well understand why the composer was driven to using it again for the last movement of one of his greatest instrumental masterpieces, the G-major violin sonata, Op. 78. As with the later "companion" songs *Sommerabend* and *Mondenschein*, *Regenlied* and *Nachklang* should be sung together.

Beneath its deceptive simplicity, *Agnes* conceals depths of Brahmsian ingenuity and feeling. Mörike's poem is the sad cry of a girl who has been forsaken by her lover. While everyone else is making merry at harvest time, she steals away to the hill where he first avowed his love for her, to be alone with her grief. The final lines of the poem, in which she speaks of the wind blowing the ribbon of her hat (that *he* gave her), are particularly touching.

The prelude to *Agnes*, though consisting of only two bars, is full of significance in that, (1) prefixed by the two time signatures 3/4 and 2/4, it tells us in advance of the song's overall five-beat pulse, (2) it begins in C minor, and (3) the rhythm of the first three chords is that of the previous *Nachklang*, suggesting that Brahms may well have composed the song with the former one still haunting his musical consciousness.

schnell vor‿bei,   bist du doch ge‿.‿gan‿.‿gen!   Wär mein Lieb   nur

Ex. 34 *Agnes*

Brahms's uncanny technical skill is shown not only in the
song's offbeat rhythm but in the way he matches the repetitions
of the poem with one-bar musical echoes and by the different
accompaniment he gives to the same melody in each verse, beginning with simple diatonic chords in unison with the voice
(folk song style) but becoming more complex and chromatic with
each verse. Like Wolf's poignant (also strophic) setting, it is in
fact a little gem of a song that grows in stature with familiarity.

With *Eine gute, gute Nacht*, Brahms joined hands with Daumer
again. The poem is typical. The lover begs his sweetheart not to
bid him goodnight and send him away when she has it in her
power to let him stay and satisfy his desire. The song may be
slight, but it fits the poem like a glove to a hand, while in its
consummate intermingling of vocal line and accompaniment it
could stand as the perfect representative of Brahms's songs from
this aspect.

The set closes superbly with *Mein wundes Herz* and *Dein
blaues Auge*. The first, by its sentiment, may be described as a
Brahms version of Schumann's famous *Widmung*. In both songs
the lover declares his worship of the loved one to be his guiding
star. Like Schumann's, Brahms's setting races along in surging
melodic arcs above hurrying right-hand quavers and a magnificent rising and falling (and sometimes canonic) bass. For the
only time in his songs, Brahms, taking a leaf out of Handel's
book, after the prelude allows the voice to make its entry unaccompanied. The first phrase is so strongly E minor that the sudden swerve towards major at "verlangt nach milder Ruh," takes
us by surprise—until we realize that the words call for the inspired modulation. The first two lines of the second verse are
treated identically with those of the first; then, at "O lächle fort,
mit deinem milden Licht," without a break the music becomes
major. The effect is like that of the sun breaking through clouds;

and with the "Mein Pol, mein Stern bist du!" the song reaches first a blazing climax and finally a *piano* close expressive of serenity born of trust. The song is so beautiful, carries us along so fast on its impassioned flow, that we have scarcely time to notice that the first bars of the melodic line are taken over by the piano, first in diminution in the treble, and then in imitation by the bass. Such casual subtlety is typical of Brahms the songwriter.

There is an ambiguity in *Dein blaues Auge* that makes for difficulty in its interpretation. The poem (by Groth again), after speaking of her wondrously beautiful deep blue eyes in which he sees mirrored his soul, then concludes by declaring that the same eyes that caused him so much grief are as cool as any lake. One asks: is it a love lyric, pure and simple, praising the loved one's beauty? Or does the "und wie ein See so kühl" contain a mordant backlash of bitterness—the *"kuhl"* implying a metaphorical coldness rather than tranquillity? Whichever the true meaning, the poem drew an exquisite song from Brahms. The prelude, with its falling two-bar melody in the right hand against the languidly rising bass, breathes languorous enchantment. The voice enters with a faint reminder, melodically and rhythmically, of Schumann.* Then, at the recollection of the pain caused by those eyes, the accompaniment loses its simple, warm E♭ harmonies and becomes more chromatic and dissonant, while the voice yearns in short, sighing cadences on the repeated "noch schmerzt," taking the music into G♭. But at the image of the cool lake, the diatonic harmonies and triads return, and with them the gentle equilibrium of the opening. The postlude repeats the prelude in a last gesture of tranquillity. The only hint that Brahms might have perceived bitterness in the final line lies in the fact that instead of what should surely have been a quiet ending, if the text is taken at face value, he has gone out of his way to mark *f* (a rare occurrence with him), as though it were an outburst of anger and resentment. The music remains the same. Only the color the singer should put into his voice can convey the requisite emotion.

By 1874, the publication year of his next volume of solo songs, Op. 63, Brahms was in his forties, and fame was coming to him surely, if slowly. But his growing reputation was being won at

---

*In particular, *Dein Angesicht.*

great cost. The Clara Schumann affair had left him emotionally drained, and had been followed by his disastrous engagement to and disengagement from Agathe von Siebold; and there had been other tentative but always abortive attachments. As early as 1862, his own city of Hamburg had rebuffed him by passing over him in favor of Stockhausen when the worthy burghers needed a conductor for their Philharmonic Society—a rebuff that rankled with Brahms for years, but which to his credit he did not allow to interfere with his friendship for the singer. His mother, whom he loved dearly, died in 1865, and he had written his *Deutsches Requiem* in her memory. His father died in 1872. He was now alone, and beginning to learn the hard ways of the world and the rough paths of love, and he was growing older.

The effects can be felt in his works composed about this time: his C-minor piano quartet, one of his most tragic works, and these Op. 63 songs. The poems he chooses to set are more and more steeped in nostalgia, in backward glances to childhood and youth. There are love songs still, to be sure, but none of the former passionate character, being mostly tinged with sad remembrance, or iridescent, as though the searing pangs of desire had been transmuted and lightened by the passage of time.

The pith and core of the songs lie in the three Groth settings given significantly the common title of *Heimweh* by the composer himself. The trio form a unity by the common substance of their theme—the backward glance, the yearning for the past— and they should be thought of and performed as a sonata in miniature: first movement, slow movement, and finale. In these terms the outer movements especially are similar in tone and style. The scenes and joys of childhood are longed for but regarded as unattainable. There is resignation alongside the nostalgic remembrances, and this is reflected in the melodies and accompaniments of all three settings. The prelude of the first ("Wie traulich war das Flecken"), with its melodious, rippling semiquavers in the left hand, sets off the song like a beautiful frame to a picture. The first two lines of the poem, if set without repetition, would have made a simple three-bar melody; but by repeating the phrase "wo meine Wiege ging," Brahms turns it surprisingly into one of five bars, thereby strengthening it. Another stroke of genius comes in the third verse, which begins as though it were to be a repetition of the first (though with a different accompaniment); but at "Mein Sehen, mein Verlangen," instead of modulating to B♭ as in the previous verses, he plunges audaciously without any preparation into the still-more-remote but warmer key of E♭, following this with a sudden return to the tonic G major in conclusion.

Number three ("*Ich sah als Knabe Blumen blühn*") is the most Schubertian song Brahms ever wrote, with echoes of *Die Taubenpost, Im Frühling*, and *Frühlingsglaube* in its warm sixths, thirds, and modulations. Yet by the subtle alchemy possessed by all great composers it remains indisputably its creator's own and is a song of great lyrical beauty in short rondo form (ABAB). But it is with the second "Heimweh" song that Brahms achieves his profoundest expression. "*O wüsst ich doch den Weg zurück*" is justly accounted among his greatest songs and among the finest in the whole literature of lieder. The poem is in part responsible for the deeper emotional tension, the sadness that is beyond tears. Some critics have disapproved of the text and ridiculed its sentimentality. This crying for the moon, this lachrymose wailing to find the way back to childhood's happy land, to the protection of mother's arm—to what end, they demand, is such maudlin self-indulgence? Without wishing to defend such poetry *per se*, I would remark that as we grow older we grow sadder, smile less, and laugh less. Any man or woman over fifty who has not been so hammered by life and circumstance that, in moments of crushing stress and strain, does not look back with nostalgic longing to the time when he or she was ignorantly happy, is fortunate indeed. Artists, by their nature more temperamental and more emotional than the generality of mankind, feel frustration, disappointment, loss, and all the other ills of life more acutely and more often than their more placid and perhaps more philosophical fellow creatures. What Johnson described as "the load of life"* presses on them more severely. And in their emotional upheavals they give expression to the bitterness, the regret, the yearning of other times, happier circumstances, before they were brought up to their dreams and desires against the callous indifference of the world in general. Thus, they lay themselves open to the charges of sentimentality, pessimism, neuroses, and what have you. The great artists, through genius and craftsmanship, can transmute their emotions, however erotic, neurotic, and

*From Boswell's *Life of Johnson*.

personal, into something universal and enduring. Now composers, being seldom literary (just as poets are seldom musical),
coming across a poem that coincides with their feeling at the
time, and liking it, will set it irrespective of its literary worth.
Schubert did this over and over again, and because he was a
genius he was able to turn the dross of the poetry into the gold
of great music. The outstanding example is arguably the mawkish
Leitner poem, *Vor meiner Wiege*, from which by consummate art
he fashioned a superbly beautiful song. In the same way, Brahms
saw in Groth's longings his own, and they drew from him one of
the most poignant of his songs. It has become all but impossible
to say anything new about this wonderful song. To analyze it
would be to paint the lily. The noble sweep of the melody; the
miraculously integrated accompaniment, with its shimmer of rising and falling diminished sevenths; the minor close in the last
verse; the postlude's final rise step by hushed step into the higher
regions of the piano until, like a vision or a dream, it dies away—
these felicities are there for all to discover and savor. No one who
has once heard the song can ever forget it.

Erinnerung, recalling past days of love and delight, by its
theme is allied with the above songs, although Schenkendorf's
poem avoids the despairing sense of loss implied in those of
Groth. Rather, its sentiment is one of rapt wonder at the power
of happy remembrance. The poet sees in imagination the places
where he and his beloved used to wander; hears again her voice
reciprocating his avowal of love; while the last lines in their
rapture seem almost to suggest a hope that such happiness may
even be experienced again. Brahms captures the atmosphere of
nostalgic delight by one of his simplest, most diatonic, and
haunting melodies developed in rondo form (ABABA).

Ex. 35 *Erinnerung*

Yet simple though the song may be, he does not fail to endow it with those subtle touches of which he was so great a master and that lift it and all such similar works above mere mechanical writing. Each return of the two melodies, for example, is given a slightly different accompaniment; while in the B episode we meet again the same magical modulatory plunge from G major (or its dominant chord) into E♭ major and back again we observed in *Heimweh* (I). With its waltz rhythm and combination of *Schmelz* and *Schmerz*, the song might have come out of the *Liebeslieder Waltzer*. It contains the quintessential Brahms.

The rest of the nine songs are love songs. The two Schenkendorf settings, *An ein Bild* and *An die Tauben*, bring Schubert to mind in their titles.* But where Heine's poem on gazing on his beloved's picture is one of grief and loss, and so set pathetically

*See *Ihr Bild* and *Die Taubenpost*, both from *Schwannengesang*.

by Schubert, that of Schenkendorf is one of longing, but hopeful longing, and Brahms reflects this in his warm, A$\flat$ harmonies and gentle melodic contours.

Though the two Tauben poems express a similarity of emotions, their respective settings are different. Where that of Schubert is translated into a lilting Viennese rhythm, that of Brahms, in its *sehr lebhaft* tempo, is turned into an exhilarating flight indicative of the bird itself, urged on by the lover to scour hill, plain, and sea in quest of his beloved to urge her to come to him and renew their separated love. The song is yet another swift and delicate one to set against the composer's many slow and sombre examples, and incidentally, a difficult one for both singer and pianist to bring off with the requisite *leggiero*.

The two *Junge Lieder* are setting's of unpublished poems by the eighteen-year-old Felix Schumann, the ill-fated son of Robert and Clara. The first, "*Meine Liebe ist grün,*" is, I suppose, to be counted among the composer's best-known songs, and it is worthy of its fame. Felix was not only the son of two of Brahms's most dearly loved friends, but his godchild, for whom he must have had special affection. The young poet's lines are radiant with a youthful, adoring love, an ecstatic rapture that in the mere thought of his beloved makes him share the passion of the nightingale. Brahms, though more than twice Felix's age, more than matches the poem's transports in his setting. The music has all the impetuosity and élan of youth, the voice's headlong sweep of melody racing above an accompaniment whose chief glory is the freedom of its bass, which, beneath tension-creating syncopations in the treble, falls and rises in impassioned arcs of sound. In this song, age joins hands with youth, the realist with the idealist, the composer with the poet.

The second *Heimweh* song, "*Wenn um den Hollunder,*" though less notable and less known, is again full of the tender emotions of young love. The lover paints in the poem a picture of himself and his sweetheart lying in each other's arms in the dusk of twilight, listening to the tolling village bell and the last song of the larks. Brahms sets the first two lines to a beautifully long-breathed melody—a typical Brahms "sentence," which the singer must not ruin by a single breath.

Ex. 36 *Wenn um den Hollunder*

The three verses being in the same mood, Brahms is vindicated in setting them strophically and conveying the languor of the lovers and the happy quietude of the scene by the sheer sensuousness of his melody. Friedländer informs us that the song was composed in the summer of 1874 and "intended as a Christmas present for the young poet and his mother." To have had his poem so beautifully and understandingly set must, one feels, have made the gift far and away the most precious of any he may have received that Christmas.

Frühlingstrost is the first song of the set, but I have deliberately left it to the end because it is not only different from the others in its mood but in its structure. The poem (by Schenkendorf) is similar in mood to the *Frühlingsglaube* of Uhland, set so magically by Schubert. But whereas Schubert is content to express tranquillity and quiet hope, Brahms takes Schenkendorf's poem by the scruff of the neck, as it were, and fills it from first bar to last with intoxicating joy. The four-bar prelude, with its racing triplets in the left hand and rising and falling octaves in the right, sets the mood and form:

Ex. 37 *Frühlingstrost*

The rising sixth (A–F$\sharp$) runs like a *leitmotif* through the song. And one should notice in passing the subtle D$\sharp$ in the voice's third bar, where one would expect the more obvious but more commonplace C$\sharp$; also that at the entry of the voice the roles of the pianist's hands are cunningly reversed. The accompaniment throughout, in fact, by its favorite Brahmsian device of "overlapping" and its heavy beat falling on the light beat of the voice, acts as a veritable springboard, stimulating, strengthening, and enhancing the vocal line and giving even greater impetus to its impassioned flow. The poem is a longish one (thirty lines), and as we have already seen in earlier instances and will see again in later ones, Brahms occasionally finds a lengthy text too testing and tends to let his music lapse in quality in the course of it. But here is no falling off, and in fact the length seems to act as a challenge to him to discover fresh means of variation, and he covers the ground like a tiger in search of prey, effortlessly and tirelessly. By shaping it as sonata-rondo form in miniature (ABACA) he gives himself greater scope.

At the C section, he modulates to D major with a change of melody and accompaniment, the latter being transformed into dancing *staccato arpeggiando quavers*. These, eight bars later, at "Wir wollen, wenn du von ihr gehst," with breathtaking craftsmanship, are made to merge (in the left hand only) into the original rhythm.

Ex. 38 *Frühlingstrost*

Following a long pause, like a held breath, the final episode plunges into an exact repeat of the first. The song, the longest in all Brahms (ten pages in the Lea Pocket Scores), blazes with unflagging inspiration from the first bar to the last, and is a masterly example of his genius for creating variety within the overall unity and unity within the variety, all bound together by an inexhaustible rhythmic virtuosity. Wolf, who, among other silly comments, criticized Brahms for being "unable to exult," cannot have been familiar with this song, nor, incidentally, many of the others, nor of the finale of his D-major symphony.

There seems to be neither rhyme nor reason in the publication dates of the songs comprised by Opp. 69, 70, 71, 72, 84, and 86. Those of Op. 69 were mostly written before those of Op. 70 and in the same month as Op. 71, while two of Op. 72's revert to as early as 1875; and while the Op. 84's belong to as late as 1882, the Op. 85's go back to 1878–79 and the Op. 86's to 1877–78. The only explanation for the jigsaw would appear to be the composer's ingrained habit of deliberately keeping back works until by revision they obtained the pass mark of his satisfaction with them.

To glance over them briefly: *Klage I* and *Klage II* are the laments of a young woman who is being forced by her father to marry against her will an elderly widower. The pathos and intensity of both poems (translations from the Bohemian by Wenzig) are completely missed by Brahms, who can do no better than setting them to uninspired limping melodies and unimaginative accompaniments. As for the Slavonic atmosphere Friedländer finds in them, to me at least it seems forced and bogus. *Tambourliedchen*, Candidus's lines about the little drummer boy, with its drum-imitation accompaniment, is more genuine and attractive, but hardly compelling. On paper *Vom Strande*, a cry of desolation from a girl's heart, looks impressive, with its *moto perpetuo* accompaniment; but closer examination soon reveals it for what it is—a theatrical gesture that fails to catch the girl's grief and is, moreover, an echo of Schumann's far-more-memorable "Das ist ein Flöten und Geigen" *(Dichterliebe)*. *Salome* aims at being "high-spirited and roguish" (Friedländer), but conveys as little of the girl's savage determination to conquer and humble her lover. The last song, *Mädchenfluch*, consists of seven pages of undistinguished, mechanical, writing purporting to interpret a poem in which a girl goes on cursing her faithless lover to her mother for thirty-six lines, now wishing he may be hanged, now drowned—wishes that only serve to cover her consuming desire to have him back, for him to become enslaved by her beauty. Not for a single bar does Brahms succeed in interpreting the passion and sensuality of the poem in musical terms. The most ardent Brahmsian can only dismiss these songs and wonder how the master could ever have allowed them to pass his stringent scrutiny.

Three among the nine songs, however, do something to mitigate the failure of the opus as a whole: *Abschied, Des Liebsten Schwur*, and *Über die See*. The first and the third may be said to complement each other, in that both are outbursts of grief caused by enforced absence from the loved one, only the first is from a man, the other from a woman. In their melodic richness, beauty, and intrinsic simplicity, both are testimonies to Brahms's power, arguably the most puissant after Handel, to convey the profoundest emotion by melody alone sustained by the barest of accompaniments. A listener totally ignorant of German and of the meaning behind the texts could not fail to catch the sense of desolation and anguish in the music. So strong, in fact, is the spell of the melodies that it is only after a more deliberate scrutiny that we become aware that the apparent simplicity of the accompaniments conceals harmonic art of the subtlest calibre and of how they give depth to the melodic line. The songs—be it said to the shame of the musical community—are so little known and the verses so short (both songs are strophic, and rightly so, thus imprinting the glorious melodies more indelibly on our memories) that I make no excuse for reproducing a complete verse of each song.

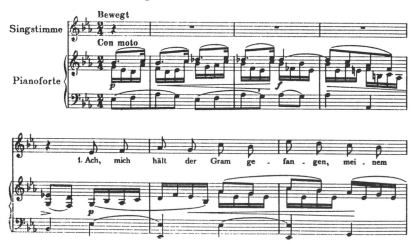

Ex. 39 *Abschied*

Ex. 40 *Über die See*

Glancing over the score, the reader will note how the bass of the prelude to *Abschied*, in counterpoint to the treble, anticipates the entry of the voice, and how the flattened D's, F's and C's deepen the harmonic tones and accentuate the poignancy of the melody.

Des Liebsten Schwur, an enchanting song, completely catches the flavor of the folk verses and brings a flood of light into the general gloom of the opus. The poem tells of a girl's clandestine meetings with her lover in the garden—clandestine because she is afraid to tell her father, who is obviously an old grump—and from it Brahms has made a song that is not only gay and attractive in itself but brings out the character of the girl in all its lovable humor. The first three verses are strophic, but for the last verse Brahms, with characteristic art, makes the prelude serve as the accompaniment and gives the voice a new melody against it. The song is a close rival to the later *Der Jäger* and makes a perfect woman's song.

Leaving Op. 69 with some relief, we now come to Opp. 70, 71, 72, 85, and 86 (the omission of Op. 84 is deliberate and to be explained later); and these, taking us from 1875–79, are contemporaneous with his first large-scale symphonic works (the first and second symphonies and the violin concerto), the first violin sonata, the two Op. 79 piano Rhapsodies, and finally, with Op. 76, the earliest of those unsurpassed lyrics for the piano that were to see their crowning consummation in the Opp. 116, 117, 118, and 119 of the 1890s. With these songs we meet with no shortcomings such as mar Op. 69; almost every song tells us we are in the presence of one of the supreme masters of the genre.

Let us look at the first song, *Im Garten am Seegestade,* in some detail, since (1) it is practically unknown and (2) it sets the tone of the songs to follow it and shows us something of the craftsmanship Brahms was now to lavish on the smallest details.

Lemcke's poem is a short, deeply-felt lyric presenting us with a picture of nature shot through with nostalgia for past happiness; its theme being that the sounds in the lakeside garden, with its old trees hiding softly-singing birds and lapping waves come to him like sad music from far-off times and fill him with nostalgic yearning. The mood of the poem is caught sensitively by Brahms in the pensive G-minor melody (at "in ihren hohen Kronen sind kaum die Vögel zu sehn" we hear an echo of the earlier "*Du sprichst, das ich mich taüschte*," Op. 32, no. 6), and still more by the accompaniment, with its interjectory descending countermelody and delicate *arpeggios* suggestive of the lapping waves.

Ex. 41 *Im Garten am Seegestade*

This countermelody immediately after "die Vögel singen Sacht" is the source of the most magical touch in the whole song; and here Brahms gives the piano this inspired interlude, which not only echoes the song of the birds in syncopated single notes but leads to a repeat of the prelude, which in turn brings a reprise of the first verse.

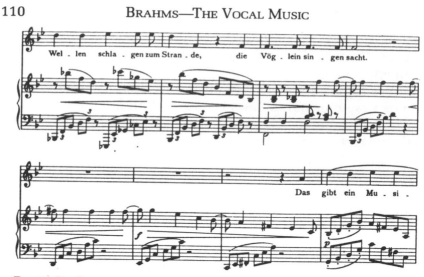

Ex. 42 *Im Garten am Seegestade*

It is details like this that declare the master hand.

With *Lerchengesang* we come to another of those masterpieces that must be the despair of any commentator. How to find words to describe a song like this? One searches for synonyms—ethereal, dreamlike, airy, insubstantial—only to find that such music defies verbal comment, beggars all description. The sentiment and rhythm of Candidus's poem clearly inspired Brahms to the utmost heights. The very first line, "Aetherische ferne Stimmen" (Ethereal far-off voices) gives him his cue: the prelude, followed by the melody, unaccompanied, seems to come floating down to us from heavenly heights.

Ex. 43 *Lerchengesang*

Then follow references to the heart rejoicing with nature, and memories of bygone times brought back by the falling dusk and singing of the late larks in the sky. On paper the song looks simple, but this is deceptive, for in fact it is one of the most difficult of all to interpret, with its exposed unaccompanied phrases, its continuous cross-rhythm against the piano (a wonderful example this is of Brahms's inexhaustible rhythmic freedom), and the uncharacteristic meagerness of the accompaniment. Yet it is these very difficulties—the tenths, octaves, and sixths high in the right hand of the accompaniment, and the nakedly unaccompanied bars—that give the song that out-of-this-world effect and vision of cerulean heights of air filled with the singing of invisible larks. Only a singer who is a good musician besides being a vocalist can hope to make its technical difficulties sound easy and achieve through sheer tonal light and shade its disembodied quality. It is not only one of Brahms's most moving songs but, like his *An eine Äolsharfe*, one of the most original, and like that song opens up new possibilities for the lied no less than the last lieder of Schubert.

The third song, *Serenade*, is I think, the only one of the composer's five Goethe settings to meet the great poet on equal ground. This may be due in part, at least, to the fact that the text is a lighthearted little snippet taken from the play *Claudine von Villa Bella*. The man sings the words, accompanying himself on the zither, to two girls, addressing each in turn as "loveliest girl," and asking them why sensitive loving souls always seem to miss happiness. The zither accompaniment, the aura of light amorous banter, and the unanswered question are caught perfectly in this charming song. Especially attractive are the fragmentary canonic accompaniment in bars 17–21, the offbeat rhythm of the melody in bar 20 and the unexpected veer into G major for the first half of bar 22.

Abendregen, the fourth and last of the "rain songs," is a not-very-satisfactory blend of different emotions, all, according to the poet, attributable to the evening rain and rainbow. Friedländer informs us that many of Brahms's friends "could not reconcile themselves to Keller's verses,* seen by them as being used by the composer as an expression of his attitude towards Wagner, with whom he had lately been corresponding. Elisabeth von Herzogenberg had even gone so far as to tease him over the last two lines with "Be satisfied with the rainbow of glory which stretches above your brow and which Portschach sees playing brightly upon your name in the dim distant future." However that may be, perhaps because of the mixed emotions and metaphors of the text, Brahms's setting, though beautiful in its individual sections—the melody of the *langsamer* section, echoed in the piano postlude, is haunting in its loveliness—does not, it seems to me, jell into a satisfactory whole. Interestingly, the piano prelude has a slight reminiscence of the early *Regenlied* discarded by the composer—another instance of unconscious memory.

Op. 71 and Op. 72 (1877) bring us a series of splendid chips from the Brahms workshop. In Heine's poem, "Es liebt sich so lieblich im Lenze!" the lovelorn shepherdess, with her garland and her longing for a young man to give it to, the background of spring flowers, and the yearning for love are all caught in the gay abandon of the fast-moving vocal line and accompaniment. With the appearance of the young horseman, who greets her but passes on without stopping, the accompaniment breaks into galloping triplets, then, with consummate art and, without stemming the music's flow, brings back the theme of the prelude first in the left hand below the triplets, now pushed into a p background, then in the right hand above them. With the final repetition of the refrainlike and now ironic title, the music takes on an even-

---

*Friedländer, *Brahms's Lieder.*

more-headlong pace, the quaver triplets breaking into four-group semiquavers racing *f* to the end of the song. Heine's rather pointless poem (entitled *Frühling*) is for once purely objective, without any trace of personal emotion, and Brahms's setting captures and enhances the objectivity.

The title of the next song, *An dem Mond*, reminds us of Schubert's four songs of that title. Brahms's setting of Simrock's poem, which asks the moon to shine on the beloved and impart all the lover's hopes and fears, is worthy of being placed with those of his predecessor. Without claiming a superlative place for it, I would nevertheless class it as a fine, atmospheric song. Its Schubertian hoverings between major and minor and its beguiling rhythm expressive of the lover's agitated longing and uncertainty against a background of moonlight and shadows. The postlude's final acceptance of the major key reflects the hope in the lover's last words.

For sheet haunting beauty, *Geheimnis* is a close rival to *Lerchengesang*. Candidus's rather silly poem, in which a lover asks the warm spring breeze, the twilight, and the opening buds if they know the *secret* (hence the title) of their love, becomes transfigured into a supreme work of art that towers above its literary origin. Here, without any effort, Brahms achieves a languorous, sensuous (but not sensual) beauty that comes and goes like a dream. When all is sheer magic, analysis would be worse than useless, but I cannot resist drawing attention to one or two salient points. Theoretically, the repetition of words and phrases in lieder is open to suspicion; for surely one of the main differences between the Lied (or art song) and the aria lies in this matter of repetition. For Handel and the classical operatic composers, for example, a couple of lines of verse are repeated ad libitum, the words being merely a frame on which to weave their musical phrases. The Lied, on the other hand, aims as a musical interpretation of the poem, paying full respect to normal stress of the words, reconciling musical phrase to the text and eschewing merely decorative interpolations. Repetition for the sake of the vocal line must be classed as such, unless done for a specific purpose. In a number of songs, Brahms, it must be admitted, lays himself open to this charge, as does Schubert no less. (Schumann, Wolf, and Fauré were more scrupulous). In this song there is probably more repetition than in any other of Brahms. "O

laues, lindes Wehn," and "was tut ihr so zusammenstehn?" in
the first verse, are both repeated, and in the second "von unsrer
Liebe süss?" is set no less than four times. Yet here, the repetition,
so far from being mechanical and reprehensible, seems even to
enhance the song. It is as if the lover, unable to credit the acceptance and return of his love, and needing to be convinced, breath-
lessly murmurs the ecstatic words to himself over and over again.
Beautiful as is the opening melody,

Ex. 44 *Geheimnis*

it becomes even more so by the slight but crucial alteration given
it on its reappearance in the second verse, where it is made even
more expressive by means of the added chromaticism and the
countermelody in the pianist's right hand.

Ex. 45 *Geheimnis*

And the final repetition of "von unsrer Liebe süss?" is one of the most moving cadences in all lieder.

Ex. 46 *Geheimnis*

No greater contrast can be imagined than that between this song and the next—*Willst du, dass ich geh?*—a contrast that like many others of a similar kind disproves the assertion made by some critics that Brahms's range of emotion and variety are less than those of the other great lieder compeers. His range is as wide as any of them, but—and here is the crux of the matter—he uses it less. I have admitted this tacitly already when I stated with reference to *Juchhe!*, *Der Frühling*, *Blinde Kuh*, and *Frühlingstrost* that such joyful, fast-moving songs make a welcome change from the far greater number of slow and sombre ones. But to any singer who complains of difficulty in compiling a group of Brahms's lieder that shall have variety, the answer is the simplest one: he does not know enough of them.

Which brings us back to *Willst du, dass ich geh?* This impassioned, almost brutally male song may be regarded as the companion piece of the more celebrated *Vergebliches Ständchen*. The lover, already in the house with his sweetheart, "traut und warm," looks out, and seeing the stormy winter night, pleads with her not to ask him to leave her to take his way home across the long miles of snow-covered moor. Like any ardent lover, he lays the climatic conditions on thick and slab, and concludes "Let me stay with you alone this night!" Unlike the *Vergebliches Ständchen*, there is no reply from the girl, the song ends abruptly with the young man's demand, and we are left to put what interpretation we will on her unspoken reply. But the song has such a headlong sweep, the lover is so eloquent in the repeated "Willst du, dass ich geh?," that it is difficult to avoid the wish and hope that he is suitably rewarded!—a wish and hope given impetus, perhaps, by the fact that for the last verse the song goes into the major. It is easy to understand why the refined Elisabeth von Herzogenberg told Brahms that the song was "quite unpleasing"* to her. Pace her opinion, it makes a splendidly virile song for a singer and accompanist who can convey its passion and intensity, and is worthy of being better known. It is also, quite incidentally, one of the most subtle examples of the composer's treatment of strophic form, so free as to approach the through-composed.

Minnelied, the last of the group, fully justifies my contention of the composer's range. It is one of the most perfect love songs ever written, and is deservedly celebrated as such. Comparison with the earlier settings of Hölty's poem by Schubert and Mendelssohn is revealing. Both those settings, in their strophic harmonic simplicity and lilting 6/8 meter, adhere more strictly, perhaps, to the poem's meter, and doubtless Goethe, who missed the whole point of what a musical interpretation of a poem

---

*Friedländer, *Brahms's Lieder.*

should be and preferred Zelter's insipid settings of his own verses to Schubert's, would have given his vote to either rather than to Brahms. Mendelssohn's version is mediocre, and Schubert's, though melodically superior, no more than ingratiating; but Brahms was obviously moved by this expression of youthful adoration, so that rhythmically, melodically, and harmonically it towers above the poem, lifting it to memorable beauty, and completely eclipses the earlier versions. The first two verses are set identically, but the shadowy nuances in the poem, suggested by the "Ohne sie is alles tot" of the third verse, is caught by the voice's and piano's fall to their lower, darker registers and the suggestion of chromaticism in the melody itself. Note here the "overlapping," the imitation between the voice and piano. For the final verse the shadows lift, and the lover's adoration blazes to its climax on the final repeated "in Wonne blühen!" The contrast between this song and those songs of uninhibited sensual suggestion to which I have referred earlier is a living proof of the range of Brahms's emotional spectrum. Here, only exquisite tenderness, love pure and ideal expressed by a warmth and beauty that raise the song to the level of the highest flights of Schumann— the composer above all other in the portrayal of the homelier moods of love. The accompaniment, though not technically difficult, demands a warm, poetical conception and a feeling for phrasing and color.

Of the five songs of Op. 72, three must be counted among the composer's greatest: *Alte Liebe, O kühler Wald,* and *Verzagen.* The text of the first, by Candidus, is dark without being depressingly gloomy. The poet welcomes the return of spring, but feels, along with its warmth and light, the shadow of an old love's bitterness, sad memories and dreams that take him back to an unfulfilled love he cannot forget. The G-minor, Brahmsian melody rises darkly above the piano's somber arpeggios; but with the reference to the warm spring morning the music veers into the major, the passage closing in E♭, only, by a magical one-bar interpolation from the piano, to be pulled back into the minor. From here the melodic line rises to a *sotto voce* lament above a chromatically falling bass. A Schubertian major/minor modulation brings the final verse into the tonic key and its first line is an exact duplication of the beginning; but at "und führt mich sene Bahn" the melody parts company with its opening and takes a downward turn expressive of the remembered sadness implied in the words, and the voice, after an agitated *crescendo*, dies plaintively away in falling and rising triads that terminate appropriately in yet another of the composer's falling sixths, to which the postlude adds a poignant farewell. With his usual critical acumen, Friedländer discerns here "a profound work which is one of Brahms's most important creations."*

A final point: the song could stand as a prime example of Brahms's art of blending accompaniment with vocal line. Without detracting from the melody, without any complex counterinterpolations, but purely by a richly suggestive harmonic flow, he adds depth to depth.

For some reason, though it is no greater than the preceding song, *O kühler Wald* is much better known. It looks simple, but as a matter of fact is deceptively complex and difficult to bring off, demanding as it does in its long, slow phrases faultless phrasing from the singer plus the rare ability to put across the shadowy unreality of the poem and Brahms's uncanny musical realization of it. For nothing is really there. The loved one, the wood she walks through, the song, and its echoes are elusive and unreal as dreams and live only in the lover's heart and memory, and the poem and the song with its rich poignant harmonies die away together like sad thoughts from a distant, irrevocable past.

After the almost static ecstasy of this song, the next— *Verzagen*—launches itself into being like a tiger.

*Friedländer, *Brahms's Lieder.*

Ex. 47 Verzagen

The grief of all humanity is expressed in this turbulent music. The scene is set on the shore, where the poet (Karl Lemcke), watching the scud of clouds and spray blown by the wind, asks why his despair cannot be dispersed like them but must eat at his heart like the restless, immovable sea. The moan and swell and surge of the waves sounds through the unrelenting, headlong rise and fall of the accompaniment, which must be one of the most difficult not only in all Brahms but in all lieder. Above it the vocal line rises and falls in mournful arches of sound, expressive of the poet's utter and unreasoning grief that can find no comfort in any philosophy or any visible solace of nature. It is a pity that this superb song is put beyond the reach of popularity by its daunting technical difficulty.

The remaining two songs, *Sommerfäden* and *Unüberwindlich*, merit only brief mention. The text of the former, by Candidus, is of a pseudo-moralistic nature in which the poet compares the gossamers he sees on the bushes everywhere with human beings. One can only wonder what moved the composer to set it at all. The melody is pensive without being memorable, with a *tour de force* of an accompaniment that if played as a solo could pass as a two-part invention of uncertain date and is, one feels, too clever by half.

The latter (a Goethe setting) is a drinking song based on a deliberate quotation from Domenico Scarlatti in which the wine bibber declares that in spite of all his attempts to conquer his passion for Love and Wine, he is as weak as water when confronted by either of them. It might, I suppose, be described as a "jolly" song and as such as far removed from being characteristic Brahms as his three drinking songs are characteristic of Schubert.

Although love songs still appear, with the twelve lieder of Op. 85 and Op. 86, we remark a growing preponderance of scene painting. *Sommerabend (II)*, together with its companion pieces *Mondenschein, Frühlingslied, In Waldeseinsamkeit,* and *Über die Heide* are all descriptive of nature and a mood, and superb descriptions at that. The first two are as atmospheric as Debussy's *Clair de Lune.* The languorous melodies and veiled *pp* accompaniments interpret Heine's nocturnes to perfection, being redolent with the glimmer of twilight and moonrise, the shimmer of still water and deepening shadows and, above all, the serenity and sense of beauty that come to the heart in quietude. Brahms's explanation for composing the songs as a pair is simple. "Both poems happen to come together in Heine's work," *(Heimkehr)* he explained to a friend. "The moon is a central figure in both, and it is very aggravating to a composer to have to use four beautiful lines only, when he might repeat them, suitably varied."* Marvelously varied they certainly are. Although both songs are complete in themselves, they should be sung as a continuous whole, for the second song is really a projection of the first, and the magic of the unexpected unison entry of voice and piano on the D♭ of *Mondenschein* after the quiet, sustained B♭ chord with which the marvelous postlude of *Sommerabend* closes, is otherwise lost. The first eight quasi-recitative bars of *Mondenschein,* in which there is to be found no tonal center, together with the *reprise* of the melody of the first song via the piano's modulations, are miracles of the composer's art at which one can never cease marveling.

*Friedländer, *Brahms's Lieder.*

Ex. 48 *Mondenschein*

And, as though these highlights of the serene beauty of the song were not enough, at the return of the original melody we are given a subtly varied accompaniment that reverses the roles of the pianist's hands and, in a consummate conclusion, a coda for the voice that soars and sinks in a wonderful arc of melody and is crowned by a postlude that, under a series of falling fifths, retraces the cross-rhythm (three against four) of the first song, to die away with an echo of the two semibreve chords that form the prelude of *Sommerabend*.

Ex. 49 *Mondenschein*

The two folk settings, *Mädchenlied* and *Ade!* are odd-men-out and lower the temperature of this otherwise original and profound set. The first, by its sad, A-minor key and natural speech rhythm (in 5/4 throughout except for the three-bar coda) does capture the Servian flavor of the poem, in which a girl laments the absence of her sweetheart, but is otherwise unremarkable. *Ade!* also is a mournful song of parting, strophic and folklike in its melodic simplicity, but given an unnecessarily elaborate and difficult accompaniment throughout of sextuplet semiquavers in the right hand against triplet quavers in the left.

Frühlingslied is not an immediately appealing song. The vocal line is full of seemingly illogical and unvocal leaps of major sevenths and similar un-Brahms-like intervals,* and the accompaniment throughout is one of continual cross-rhythm of four quavers in the right hand against remorseless triplets in the left in addition to imitation and syncopation. It is in fact one of the most difficult of songs to fix in the mind and even more difficult to bring off in performance, being one of those examples in which the instrumental composer tends to swamp the songwriter. But I implore singer and pianist not to let this put them against the song, for with perseverance they will find it to be a song of radiant clarity and deeply expressive of the lover's hope and longing: and more, one of the outstanding examples of that unrivaled rhythmic freedom of Brahms to which I have referred more than once. The piano part especially is a triumph of harmonic, melodic, and rhythmic genius. One typical example is the way in which the descending syncopated chords in the *animato* bars (19 and 20) become transformed into their equivalent ascending progression in the short postlude, giving a sense of almost uncontrollable joy and hope and love.

With *In Waldeseinsamkeit* we touch the heights of *Lerchengesang* again. In considering this song, it is all but impossible not to call to mind one of Fauré's most exquisite Mélodies, *En Sourdine*. The similarity of mood, situation, and even texture is striking. In both, the poems (the German by Lemcke, the French by Verlaine) depict two lovers lost to the world in the falling dusk and wrapped around by lonely silence and shadowing trees. In both, the atmosphere engendered by the poem is superbly cap-

*See *Example 1.*

tured. In both, the ending is personified in the distant song of
the nightingale. Both in fact are tone poems. But in Verlaine
the nightingale is the voice of "notre désespoir";* in Lemcke of
rapture. So with Fauré the inexpressibly beautiful vocal line
closes on "chantera," with a falling octave above an arpeggio
accompaniment that remains harmonically unresolved for three
bars until coming to its resolution in the final one. With Brahms,
following the exquisite major/minor ambivalence of the repeated
"ferne," the "sang eine Nachtigall" closes first on the falling triad
of B major then, repeated; on a rising third above a flowing cantabile counterpoint from the piano. This ethereal close on the full
tonic chord perfectly conveys the rapturous embrace of the lovers
in the hush of the twilight. It is, moreover, a perfect example of
Brahms's genius in the blending of vocal line and individual
accompaniment—the latter having its own ravishing countermelody.

Ex. 50 *In Waldeseinsamkeit*

It would be interesting for a singer to sing the two songs one
after the other as a comparison between masterpieces of two of
the greatest exponents of the art of song—the one so German,
the other so French.

Feldeinsamkeit, one of the most celebrated of all the songs,

*Poem by Verlaine, *En Sourdine.*

and the less known *Über die Heide*, are both tone poems, the one of summer, the other of autumn. The sense of rapturous contemplation, of floating on a sea of beauty above the cares of the world, as though all spirit, has never been so wonderfully expressed as in the former song. The warm p F-major chords seem to rise from earth across the horizon above the static bass octaves like the clouds followed by the eyes of the poet as he lies lost in thought in the grass, and the dreamy melody, so subtly varied and magically harmonized in the second verse with its atmospheric unisons, carries the listener on it until, like the poet, he feels himself "subsumed in the marvelous universe."*

The somber atmosphere of autumn sadness and lost love is no less caught in Storm's *Über die Heide* than the dreamy somnolence of summer in *Feldeinsamkeit*. An almost sinister atmosphere broods over this powerful song in which Brahms reveals a new and astonishing terseness and economy. The hollow sounding steps of the wanderer, the mist, the moor, the gray empty sky, are all suggested by the stark, repetitive bass octaves, the syncopated G-minor chords, and the vocal line with its lugubrious, cramped intervals. In the postlude, with its rising melody against a falling bass, we hear and almost visualize the lonely, disillusioned wanderer fade into the autumnal mist out of sight and sound. The poignancy and somber mood depicted here both in the poem and music recall the *Winterreise* songs; and indeed this song measures up to those masterpieces and would not be out of place among them.

Therese, a poem by Keller, is all but unintelligible unless one knows the background to it. The poem is one from a set describing the crescendo and diminuendo of the love of a young man for an older, more experienced woman who, after first spurning him, realizes she has been hoist with her own petard and, too late, tries to win him back. So much understood, the song makes much more sense; and relishing its subtlety, one asks oneself in some despair why Brahms did not set the rest of the poems and make a cycle with them. Expressive as they are of the varying moods of love, they would surely have drawn from him some-

---

*Allmer's own words in a letter to a publisher protesting that Brahms's setting of his poem failed to please him! This is only another instance of the nonmusical writer's intransigence and inability to appreciate genius in a different art. Other notable examples are Goethe, Daudet, and Housman.

thing better than the shadowy narrative of the *Magelone Romanzen*. Following the five-bar prelude, the first two verses are
set strophically in Brahms's folk song vein; but for the final verse,
after an ambiguous piano interlude closing in F♯ major (the tonic
key is D), both melody and accompaniment take on a Wolfian
complexity, its overall tonality never settling until the end of the
postlude, suggestive of the woman's deliberate mystification of
her naive young man. Like *Am Sonntag Morgen*, the song anticipates Wolf in its concentrated, mordant subtlety.

With *Versunken*, Felix Schumann provided his godfather with
a third and last text. "I am drowning in seas of love! Everything
is mine—the sun, the stars, the rainbow, the world!" The music,
I think, does not altogether match the young poet's ecstatic rapture, being stormy rather than rapturous, and the *leidenschaf-
tlich* turbulence seems rather self-conscious and forced.
Certainly the song is not as attractive and interpretative as the
two earlier settings of the young Schumann.

We come finally to two masterworks: *Nachtwandler* and *Todessehnen*. The former poem, by Kalbeck, holds a symbolic meaning rather along the lines of *Blinde Kuh*. Brahms's setting
completely invokes the atmosphere of the poem and interprets
it in musical terms with uncanny insight. The smooth rise and
fall of the prelude's bass, the rocking movement of the treble,
and the interchange of major/minor tonality create a chiaroscuro
of nocturnal light and shadow with the sleepwalker gliding
through it like a ghost.

Ex. 51 *Nachtwandler*

There is a dream aura, too, in the melody itself, which rises and falls softly above a syncopated accompaniment. The first two verses are strophic, but the third is yet another example of Brahms's genius in variation. "Still in seinen Traum versunken" is set to melody with little movement, while the accompaniment is no other than the prelude itself—an inspired stroke.

Ex. 52 *Nachtwandler*

At the final line the melody climbs an octave, only to fall back into the lower register of the voice and close on G (the dominant note of the tonic key), unresolved by the accompaniment, which for postlude repeats the prelude, conjuring up the picture of the sleepwalker returning unawakened to the darkness whence he came. The song achieves the maximum effect with the minimum of means, and one may say of it, as also of so many of Schubert's songs, that nothing like it had been attempted before. The aura of the spectral and the subconscious that pervades the song makes it unique among Brahms's lieder, only to be equaled by Schubert's *Der Doppelgänger*.

Finally, *Todessehnen*. Why, one asks, did Brahms, the agnostic, set a poem that is not only a cry from the depths for death but also an appeal to the *"Vater in der Höhe"* to take the poet from life to the place "where Life and Love are one?" In other words, the text is in the broadest sense religious, an affirmation—if a morbid one—of belief in something beyond the grave. Whatever the composer's thought on the sentiment of the text, his setting is a splendid one, utterly transcending it. The low tessitura, allied with the mournful, F♯-minor key, makes it a superb song for any bass who is prepared to explore these depths, and the accompanist can delight in the Wolf-like richness and chromaticism of the piano writing. The melody of the second half (*langsam*, F♯ major), with its flowing accompaniment, was to be echoed in the *Più adagio of the Andante* of the B♭ piano concerto.

I have deliberately withheld comment on the Op. 84 *Romances and Songs for One or Two Voices* for two reasons: (1) they were almost certainly written later than the Op. 85 and Op. 86 sets and (2) they stand apart from them in that, as their title forewarns, they consist of those essentially German duologues between "Mutter" and "Tochter" or "Er" and "Sie," which have little appeal today. Yet it is typical of nineteenth-century taste in general and of Brahms's friends in particular that they should rave over these folksy lightweights and disparage or ignore masterpieces like *Verzagen* and *Willst du, dass ich geh?* With two notable exceptions, the five songs (*Sommerabend (I)*, *Der Kranz*, *In der Beeren*, *Vergebliches Ständchen*, and *Spannung*) cannot compare with the similar examples Brahms had already given us with *Liebestreu* and *Von ewiger Liebe*. Only *Der Kranz* has urgency and depth, while the humor and deftness of *Vergebliches Ständchen* have made it one of the most popular of all his songs. It may in fact be described as the feminine version of *Willst du, dass ich geh?* The lover outside pleads with his *inamorata* to let him in, but he is sent away with a flea in his ear for his male-chauvinist audacity. When setting the text, Brahms was under the impression (an impression perpetuated for future generations by the many editions of the song) that it was a Niederrheinisches Volkslied and unaware that the archdeceiver composer-poet Zuccalmaglio had completely rewritten it. Not that this matters when it comes to the music. Here we have what is one of Brahms's most original settings of folk poems (or poems in the Volkslied tradition). No suppression here of his own unique composer-spirit in order to preserve folk-song simplicity, as there had been with some of his earlier attempts. This is unadulterated Brahms, and posterity has taken it to its heart. The racy melody and accompaniment catch the very spirit of the racy dialogue. In the lover's second appeal, Brahms conveys the feeling of the cold night wind and the dark simply by taking the melody into the minor and giving it an onrunning accompaniment of unisons; while for the girl's clinching finale he returns to the major, but adds a more intricate harmonization to the climax in an expressive postlude, in which we can hear her scornful, dismissive slam of the window in her crestfallen lover's face. In view of the different interpretations given to the girl's final "Gute Nacht, mein Knab!," singers would do well to make a mental note to the effect that the composer insisted that her mood was one of haughty outrage, not regret. In contrast to Wolf, Brahms was not given to paeans of praise of his own songs; nevertheless, he was proud of this song, as well he might be. In reply to Hanslick's congratulations on it he wrote, "It gives me great pleasure to thank you for your letter, for it was really something special for me, and I am in a particularly good humor about it. . . . For this one song I would sacrifice all the others. . . ."

Following the appearance of these lieder in 1882, Brahms was not to publish another song until 1884.

6

The Later Songs

With these songs, mostly composed in the mid-1880s, we approach the final phase of the composer's creative life. These thirty-seven songs bring us masterpiece after masterpiece, with fewer and fewer that can be passed over as dispensable. Age and maturity combine with ever-increasing originality and craftsmanship to achieve a more subtle realization of his aims and a corpus of work that anticipates the clarinet chamber music and the last piano works. Harmonically, the songs tend towards simplification allied with more daring shifts and loosening of tonality along with an even greater clarity of texture,* all combining to create deeper intensity and making them still more varied, more individual. Being the incomparable melodist he is, he does not sacrifice melody; but from now on the equally great harmonist and creator of free, future-anticipating rhythms comes more and more into play. Songs like *Mit vierzig Jahren, Steig auf, geliebter Schatten, Meerfahrt, Nachtigall, Auf dem Kirchhofe*, and *Es hing der Reif* would have been impossible at any earlier stage.

Moreover, there is an external significant pointer to the impassioned songs of this period, namely, his love for the young singer, Hermine Spies. Talented, attractive, and not backward in showing her admiration for the fifty-year-old composer, she obviously held him in thrall. Some of the songs reveal such warmth of feeling that his friend Theodor Billroth wrote in a letter to the composer that he suspected a secret passion behind their crea-

---

*Or as Sibelius perceptively put it: "Brahms became clearer in his old age." Quoted by Bernard Jacobson in his *The Music of Johannes Brahms* (London: Tantivy Press, 1917).

tion. He was right. It was the Agathe affair over again; and as with her, Brahms made his escape while expressing his passion in his music.

The very first song of Op. 94, *Mit vierzig Jahren*, is the one that so moved Julius Stockhausen when he first sang it with Brahms at the piano, that he broke down. Rückert's poem, a cry of age that, looking back from the watershed of life, sees youth in the valley behind gone forever, and the uncertain descending track before," was made for Brahms, and his perception of this speaks in every bar. In terms of form it stands arguably as the most perfect example of that amalgam of the strophic and the through-composed that Brahms made so uniquely his own. From the prelude with its opening dotted rhythm on the dominant to the final chord of the postlude it is one of the most highly organized of all the songs. Whole phrases are repeated from verse to verse, but always with the subtlest of variation. Every nuance of the poem is caught. When a whole song is masterly, it may seem superfluous to select examples, but I cannot resist drawing attention to the passage at "Hindehnt ein Bergesrücken sich," just before the final verse, where the right hand falls chromatically against the left hand's chromatically rising line, to be followed by the ensuing bleak unisons with the voice,* expressive of the unknown journey and destiny ahead. Note, too, the one-bar enharmonic modulation in preparation for the last verse, and finally, the unexpected modulation to the major together with the sudden smoothing of the melody and the upward flowing triplets of the accompaniment, changing the previous gray atmosphere to one of, if not actual hope, at least resignation. The effect is like that of the sun breaking through the mist, a harbor reached after a storm. At the final "bist du im Port," the voice sinks with a valedictory gesture to a full close; but with its rising arpeggios and final major chords the postlude seems to call the symbolic traveler to the vistas ahead. The song repays endless study, and emerges more subtle and profound with every hearing. And indeed, when one has thoroughly absorbed this wonderfully constructed and emotive song, one begins to understand why Stockhausen broke down.

Steig auf, geliebter Schatten is a terse, elusive song of the utmost intensity, like the text. Halm's poem might have been writ-

*See Example 12.

ten by Emily Brontë, having all the rhythmic simplicity and power of her greatest poems; her directness combined with ambiguity of thought; her sense of challenge to Love, Life, Fate, Pain, or what you will; and her appeal for consolation while in the same breath condemning weakness and refusing to allow the spirit to break under the strain. Who or what is the beloved Shadow that, living or dead, can bring strength and comfort to the poet, we cannot tell here any more than in the similar evocations of Emily Brontë. The Shadow remains inscrutable—a shadow, and no more. Brahms's setting is perfect in its musical interpretation, charged with meaning that cannot be pinned down, with overtones that escape; goes depth beyond depth. His favorite tragic key of E♭ minor forebodes this, and the right-hand broken chords, together with the emotive, constantly recurring falling phrase in the left hand, anticipating the voice and becoming almost a *leitmotif*, confirm it. Brahms's bass, always free, is superb here.

Ex. 53 *Steig auf, geliebter Schatten*

The form is ternary, and for the middle section the music, catching on to the "Du hasts gekonnt im Leben, du kannst es auch im Tod," goes into the relative major, opening up vistas of hope. But the final verse repeats the first, and the brief postlude falls into the dark, lower regions of the piano as though the summoned ghost itself was returning into the shadows from which it came.

The next two songs, *Mein Herz ist schwer* and *Sapphische Ode*, though poles apart in mood and organization, have one thing in common: Brahms's favorite device of syncopation to depict emotion and at the same time to ensure the rhythmic flow. The former song conveys the nostalgia and hopelessness in Geibel's poem, first by fast-moving, rising and falling octaves in contrary motion in the piano, and later by richly scored harmonies exemplified by a series of unresolved 7th chords. The song closes with a reversed repetition of the poem's first two lines, the music being a varied echo of the opening melody—a telling stroke.

But the syncopated accompaniment of the latter song, given a *Ziemlich langsam* tempo, serves to accentuate the dreamy passion of one of the most famous love songs ever written. It has all the Brahms fingerprints: the restless syncopations; the pedal points; the slight but telling variation in the second verse; and above all the long-breathed, glowing vocal line with its falling and rising triads so expressive of the poignant lines of the text, making it, like Schubert's *Du bist die Ruh'*, one of the most testing of songs. How right Brahms was in his choice of tessitura here! Only the richest contralto voice can do it justice. Any transposition would be as unforgivable as that for Bach's "Have mercy upon me, O Lord" or Handel's "He was despised."

The brusque contrast of *Kein Haus, keine Heimat*, comes almost like a physical blow. This is Brahms's shortest song (only twenty bars in all, one shorter than the early *Heimkehr*) and must be one of the briefest ever written. Halm's poem, the defiant cry of a homeless, family-less, friendless tramp who throws his condition in the face of society with a gesture of bravado, must call up in the minds of English listeners the similar *The Vagabond* of R. L. Stevenson, so splendidly set by Vaughan Williams. The only criticism one can make of Brahms's powerful, strident setting is that it is all over before the listener can absorb it: it is almost too brutally terse.

Coming to the seven songs of Op. 95, we find ourselves confronted by a query. Of them, Friedländer states that "In contrast to the preceding Op. 94, whose five numbers are written for a male voice, the following, with one exception, are girl's songs (*Mädchenlieder*).* But this must be a slip. Numbers 2, 3, and 7

*Friedländer, *Brahms's Lieder*.

are clearly for a male singer. The text of the first, *Das Mädchen*, is a translation from the Serbian; and apart from a slightly Serbian accent and an unusual rhythmic pulse in alternating 3/4 and 4/4 meter, the song is not a memorable one. But *Der Jäger*, makes a perfect genre concert piece. The girl comes to life in the three strophic verses. She knows her womanizing lover through and through. He's a hunter, she says, but a hunter of girls too, and is on her trail; but she is not falling for his charms and blandishments so easily. It is the church door or nothing for her! One can almost see the roguish smile and the self-assured toss of her head in the racy vocal line and the dancing accompaniment. *Vorschneller Schwur* is another Serbian folk translation. The girl makes a vow that she will not be enticed any more by a lover's words and caresses, but immediately repents her rashness. Brahms's setting is indifferently authentic and does not rise above pleasant mediocrity. But the *Mädchenlied* of Heyse is, again, pure Brahms. As she washes her clothes in the stream, the girl declares: "When I die and find myself in heaven, the first thing I shall do is to look for my lover. If he's not there I shall go back to sleep for ever and ever. It wouldn't be heaven without him!" The song is a charmer, capturing the lovable simplicity of the girl completely—the Brahms equivalent of those little gems of Schubert and Schumann, *Seligkeit* and *Volksliedchen*.

The remaining three songs of the set, for male voice are *Bei dir sind meine Gedanken*, *Beim Abschied*, and *Schön war, das ich dir weihte*. The text of the first, by Halm, is not easy to translate into equivalent English, being ambiguous, not to say enigmatic. "My thoughts hover around you, tell you I am homesick and full of longing for you; but those same thoughts tell me that there wings are singed by the power of your glances" is a literal translation. Brahms gives to the indeterminate mood of the poem music, which, while fast-moving and light, conceals depths of tenderness; and the accompaniment alone, a rippling duet between the pianist's hands, fully conveys the image of loving thoughts fluttering around the distant loved one, making the strophic song a joy either to listen to or perform.

Beim Abschied exemplifies the composer's endless self-criticism and search for perfection. Halm's poem is a text of ten lines with feminine endings in which the lover expresses his contempt for the idle chatterers around him, absorbed as he is by

the coming separation between him and the "One who matters."
Brahms made two settings, the second merely a slight variation
of the first, the only difference being that for the first half of the
original version the 3/8 melody is given a dancing accompaniment in the same beat, somewhat reminiscent of Schubert's *Der
Musensohn.*

Ex. 54 *Beim Abschied*

Only for the second half of the verse does the accompaniment
slide wickedly into a 2/4 cross-rhythm against the voice. Then,
as so often with Brahms, second thoughts came into play; and
perceiving that the conflict of rhythms gave a more restless and
mordant flavor to the song and moreover brought out the clash
between the lover's feelings for the One and his impatient indifference for the crowd around him, he decided to let the cross-
rhythm permeate the song. Thus, instead of beginning it as in
the previous example we now get.

kanns nicht verschmer - zen und kanns nicht ver - win - den in mei - nem Her - zen,

Ex. 55 *Beim Abschied*

Again it exemplifies to perfection Browning's "Oh, the little more, and how much it is!"

With *Schön war, das ich dir weihte* we come to the penultimate Daumer setting. Technically the song is perhaps the best example in all Brahms for its flagrant indifference to the stresses and overall construction of the poem. The phrase "das goldene Geschmeide," with its heavy accent on the final "de" is as bad as the notorious "*Königin.*" With skill, a singer may soften such defects; but the singer cannot obviate the thoroughly bad construction here that forces the rhymes into the middle of the musical phrases (e.g., *beide* and *Geschmeide, gewesen* and *auserlesen*). Yet despite such heinous offences, with skill and conviction an intelligent signer can make an impressive song of it, for there is no little profundity here. For the music, with its heavily charged, syncopated bass line, minor key, and broken melodic phrases unmistakably matches the dark mood of the poem. It will be observed that, unusual for Brahms, the right hand of the accompaniment follows the voice for the greater part of the song. This was surely done with intention to give more weight to the melody. Only at "empfangen einen bessern Lohn," where the voice rises and falls in a passionate arch of anguished protestation, do melody line and accompaniment part company, underlining the rift between the lovers.

Op. 96 set was originally intended to contain only settings of Heine, the Daumer being added later. The three Heine poems are taken from the cycle *Die Heimkehr*, from which, with the *Sommerabend* and *Mondenschein* of Op. 85, Brahms had already fashioned two masterpieces. Now he was to surpass even those. More than one writer has maintained that *Der Tod, das ist die kühle Nacht* is Brahms's supreme song, and there is good reason for their contention. Formally, melodically, harmonically, and in its musical interpretation of every nuance of the poem, it vindicates its claim for a place among the supreme songs of the world. Even more than with *Mit vierzig Jahren,* one can understand why a performer or listener should be moved to tears. Emotionally, it seems to sum up the experiences of a lifetime, to color the day-end of life with all the hues of sunset. Love, remembrances, and the song of the nightingale come to the tired would-be sleeper from infinite distances, like dreams. To bring cold analysis to bear on such a poem and song would be indeed to gild refined gold. Enough to say that everything the composer had to give is to be found here: the slow, langorous melody; the rich, chromatic harmonies; the magical modulations; the pedal-point bass; the dreamy, arpeggio chords blending with the voice; the piano interjections either anticipating or imitating the melodic line; the languourous upward-moving arpeggios suggestive of rising tides of darkness; and finally the postlude summoning an infinitely moving farewell to the evanescent loveliness in five *träumerisch* bars that die away into silence like the last heartbeats of a departing spirit.

The fourteen-bar prelude to *Meerfahrt,* the longest and one of the most eloquent of all the songs, sets the scene and invokes the sinister atmosphere of the song.

Ex. 56 *Meerfahrt*

The unexpected *f* passages convey an atmosphere of foreboding and menace; the shifting tonality with its gropings for the home key suggests the helpless drifting of the boat with its two forlorn lovers sailing over a trackless sea; the mournful melody is eloquent of despair; and the unceasing rising and falling triplet rhythm suggests the swell of the sea over which they are journeying. Probably because few singers can do it justice, the song is not as widely known as it should be. Nevertheless it is one of the greats.

The third Heine song, *Es schauen die Blumen*, though ingratiating, is light-weight in comparison. The text is yet another of Heine's lachrymosities. (In passing, and recalling *Dichterliebe*, *Am Meer*, *Ihr Bild* among many others, one may be forgiven for marveling at the ease with which this poet shed his *Tränen*). Here he sends his beloved flowers and with them his songs with their "Tränen und Seufzer." Through-composed, the song stresses the flowers rather than the sighs and tears, the two verses being given a flowing *cantabile* melody with a tricky, typical Brahms cross-rhythm accompaniment of two-against-three semi-quavers marked "Unruhig bewegt," which wars with rather than deepens the melody. For the conclusion of the second (and last) verse, by changing the bass from its straight two-beat pulse to a single syncopated pedal B and a repeat of the final line "ihr Lieder wehmütig und trüb" at half the tempo, plus a sustained high F♯ for the "trüb," Brahms does induce a certain wistfulness; but it hardly matches the poet's sentimental grief. It is, I repeat, an ingratiating song, but hardly comparable with the others.

One can only feel pleasure that Brahms decided to include his ultimate Daumer song, so crowning a series of masterly settings of that indifferent poet through which, like Schubert with his Müller, he has given him the accolade of immortality. *Wir wandelten* is, after *Wie bist du, meine Königin*, perhaps the best known of the Daumer songs, even of all the songs. Yet again, recalling

Meerfahrt, one can only marvel at the range of Brahms's technique and emotional gamut. There, all was sinister, symbolic gloom, desolation, and heartbreak. Here, we are presented with the profoundest possible contrast. Again we have two lovers; but far from voyaging forlornly over trackless seas, they wander (hand in hand, one feels) in solitude and silence, lost in their own thoughts. He wonders what her thoughts are. His own, he confesses, are serene with a lover's happiness, chiming in his mind like little golden bells, and so blissful that they surpass in beauty all earthly sounds. To say that the song is technically faultless; to note the counterpoint, slipped unobtrusively into the prelude like a sleight of hand; to draw attention to the magic of the modulation from A♭ to E halfway through the song; to admire the inspired melodic line and the subtly blended accompaniment— all these are aspects of its greatness. But what above all gives the song its stature is not so much the details, important though they are, as the integral blending of words and music to create an atmosphere of rare tranquillity, peace, and physical and mental harmony between the lovers as, with their separate, introvert, unspoken thoughts, they wander idly together. That is the supreme achievement of this wonderful song.

Much the same comment applies to the first of Op. 97—yet another supreme song—*Nachtigall.* Like *Lerchengesang,* with which it is comparable, it is one of the composer's most original and ethereal creations. As I remarked earlier, a scene painting in a poem rarely failed to bring out the highest degree of inspiration from Brahms. In the nightingale's song, the poet hears not just the notes themselves, but a faint echo of even diviner sounds, a voice from heavenly far-off regions. The prelude not only conjures up the bird's plaintive song and background of woodland solitude, but lays out the basic rhythm of the lied.

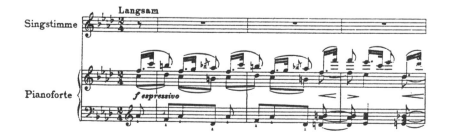

Ex. 57 *Nachtigall*

The melodic line takes over this rhythm in short, quasi-recitative phrases: but at "Nein, trauter Vogel," as though borne up by the poet's deepening emotion, it buds and blossoms into an ever-rising, upward-reaching melody.

Ex. 58 *Nachtigall*

Then, in a master touch, on the repeated "ein leiser Widerhall" the music dies away in the major like an echo of an echo. The subtlety of the last three bars of the accompaniment, with its

rising *arpeggiando* and its countermelody in the right hand echoes by the left, all consummated in the final *pp*, rippled F-major
chord, will repay endless study.

Ex. 59 *Nachtigall*

No postlude is needed after this.

Auf dem Schiffe, by its complete contrast, is yet another illustration of the range of Brahms's art to which I have already referred. The poem (if such a naive versicle can be designated as
such) merely expresses the wish of the poet to be like the bird
he sees from a boat on the Rhine, and to be able to soar and
skim over the water in abandoned freedom. Here is the perfect
example of the style of poem that can provide the composer
with the basic essentials for the creation of song: rhyme, rhythm,
simplicity, the painting of a scene, and invocation. Brahms found
all the ingredients he needed in the jingle to give him the springboard from which to take off. A *lebhaft und rasch* introduction,
with its dancing semiquavers, gives us an almost onomatopoeic
picture of the bird (a swallow, one feels), flying now high, now
low, over the river. The voice then joins with the piano in a light,
fast-moving 3/8 rhythm. From beginning to end the song is an
irresistible, infectious revel of gay abandon, and a gift to singer
and pianist alike.

Entführung, a short Herder-like ballad of abduction, together
with *Dort in den Weiden* and *Trennung*, both in strophic, volkslied style, can be passed over with bare mention. The two latter
are no improvement on the versions included in the 49 *Deutsche
Volkslieder*, and one is driven to wonder why Brahms went to
the trouble of resetting them. *Komm bald*, however, takes us to a
higher plane altogether. It is another of the world's most beautiful
love songs, lyrical, tender, and warm. The poem, by Groth, expresses the lover's longing in the absence of his beloved, from
his garden and the friends come to see him. The lovely, "viola"

melody steals into being between the pedal points of "violin" and "cello." Note the out-of-key hovering on dominants between E and A major, the little quaver group, destined to play so important a part both in the harmonic figurations and in the melody itself (a thematic exemplar worthy of the great Haydn, master of masters in this respect), which leads into the vocal line.

Ex. 60 *Komm bald*

Of the four brief verses the first two are strophic, but for the third and fourth Brahms conjures up new melodies, which are in fact variations. The modulations towards the end of the second strophe, hinting in turn at C major, F major, and A minor, and so back to the E-major prelude, expressive of the dreamlike unreality felt by the singer, are enchantingly beautiful. In the final verse Brahms illustrates the axiom that every melody must have a culminating point by taking the voice up to high G on the "mir" of "und mir geblieben." The repeated "wärst du, wärst du dabei!," with its final phrase referring to the little quaver rhythm, catches all the wistfulness of the lover longing for the return of the one who means more to him than the rest of the world. In addition to the sheer melodic and harmonic loveliness of the song, it is one of the supreme examples of Brahms's unsurpassed skill in the handling by variation of the basically simple strophic form. As a point of interest, the poet had sent the composer a manuscript copy of his poem as a tribute on the latter's fifty-second birthday. By the next day Brahms had set it and sent a copy to Hermine Spies.

With the opus numbers in the hundreds, we come towards the end of Brahms's career as a composer of lieder, and it is a magnificent ending. Opp. 105, 106, and 107 form, with few exceptions, worthy companions to the last piano and chamber music works. The text of Wie Melodien zieht es mir, by Groth, is an elusive little poem, as one would expect, since its theme is the elusiveness of words and rhymes for the poet which come and go like melodies, intangible and fugitive as dreams. Brahms's rising and falling melody spans the first two lines like a noble arch over the chancel of a cathedral. (See Example 8.) Again the song is strophic in principle but subtly varied with each verse. The singing cello-like bass line seems to create both harmony and melody. The marvelous passage towards the end—so expressive of the wistful words and its groping, as it were, for the tonic key through unrelated flat keys, together with the final falling phrase of the voice and the brief but eloquent postlude—conveys perfectly that pensive introspection that is close to those tears that the poet envisaged, the secret of which is held only by the greatest masters. Some writers purport to find resemblances to the song in the first movement of the A-major violin sonata written contemporaneously, but there is no more than a slight subconscious affinity of key and melodic shape.

The various Mädchenlieder and songs written specifically for female singers that occur in all stages of Brahms's songwriting career vary enormously in quality. Some (Liebestreu, Der Schmied, Wiegenlied, Von waldbekränzter Höhe, Therese, Der Jäger, and Vergebliches Ständchen) are among either the most well-known or greatest of the songs; others (Die Liebende schreibt, Liebesklage des Mädchens, Vom Strande, Mädchenfluch, and others) must be counted among the comparative failures, or dispensable ones. Now, towards the end of his life, Brahms was to give us three that take their place among his finest and most characteristic songs: Immer leise wird mein Schlummer, Das Mädchen spricht and Mädchenlied (Op. 107, no. 5).

I observed that Der Tod, das ist die Kühle Nacht is arguably Brahms's greatest song. Immer leise also, could well stake a claim for that accolade. The composer's friend, Theodor Billroth, in his reply to Brahms acknowledging receipt of a copy of the song, wrote: "The poem of the dying girl by H. Lingg and your setting thrilled me. . . . I am, not ashamed to confess that I could not finish playing it for my tears.* No one who has played or sung or heard a performance of this saddest of sad songs will be surprised by Billroth's confession. Both the poem and Brahms's setting are expressions of sheer, naked emotion, and it is impossible either to perform or listen to the song without being moved. The girl knows she has not long to live, knows that her lover will eventually seek consolation elsewhere. All she asks is that, before she goes, before May returns with its bees and thrushes, warm days and new hopes, he will knock at her door for a last time. And she ends her wish and the song with an agonized cry of "Komm, o komme bald!" But the "Come soon!" is something very different from the earlier song of that title. There, it is only the plaintive sigh of a lover over the temporary absence of his beloved. Here, it is the anguished cry from the heart of one who knows that her cry may never be answered. There is no prelude; the voice enters pp without any preamble in a murmured acceptance of the inevitable, emphasized by the thirds and sixths of the right hand, while the left repeats the rhythm like muffled drum taps.

Ex. 61 *Immer leise wird mein Schlummer*

The girl dreams over and over again that her lover has knocked on her door, but no one has answered, and the voice becomes a

*Friedländer, *Brahms's Lieder.*

wistful melody followed by short, interrupted phrases as though
the memory were too painful to be borne, while the accompaniment takes the harmony through rich modulations—E, G, F, E
minor—before the close of the first verse in the home key (C♯
minor) on the voice's eloquent "weine bitterlich"—the first climax. With that subtlety of variation so characteristic of Brahms's
genius, the vocal line of the first verse is given to the piano as a
prelude to the second. The wizard waves his wand and the same
becomes different. The chilling "eine Andre wirst du küssen,
wenn ich bleich und kalt" takes the voice into the dark, alto
regions, made even darker by the piano's sequence of sixths in
the lower register. At the girl's vision of the summer that she will
not live to see, the "dream melody" of the first verse returns,
only to be followed by the second and final climax. The interrupted gasped phrases return, rising higher and higher through
G major and B♭ to the consummating, enharmonic D♭ major on
the anguished "O komme bald!" over the piano's agitated right-
hand syncopations and left-hand arpeggios. The song ends with
a repeat of the "Komm, o komme bald!," dying away to a murmur
as though the singer were exhausted by the effort; and the postlude, in resigned syncopations, drops the curtain on the scene.

The whole of this passage is so original and moving that I
cannot resist quoting it in full, even though the song is well-
known and admired.

Ex. 62 *Immer leise wird mein Schlummer*

Summing up, one may say of the song that it displays all the *Angst* of the Romantics, expressed with a technique as controlled as that of the great classical masters.

Das Mädchen spricht is one of the happiest and most lovable songs in all Brahms. The girl, about to become a bride, can't restrain her joy, which overflows in converse with the swallow she sees sitting in her new nest. "Is your mate an old love, or a new?" she asks. "Are you, like me, a bride?" Her almost incoherent happiness comes across to us in the jaunty falling and rising melody, with its short-breathed phrases enhanced by the delicate tracery of the beautifully interwoven accompaniment, with its displaced rhythms, its modulatory plunges into the keys of C and F, and its typically Brahms variation for the first half of the second verse. The song is the last strophic one Brahms was to write, and a triumphant vindication of his unfaltering faith in the form. It is as well a sheer joy to perform for both singer and pianist.

The last, *Mädchenlied* (Op. 107, no. 5), a combination of *volks-lied* simplicity and Brahmsian subtlety, crowns them all. The girl at her spinning wheel laments that she is the odd one out. The others have their lovers and are spinning for their dowry. She alone is without a lover and can take no joy in her work. The mournful, B-minor melody sings above a continual rising and falling *arpeggiando* accompaniment suggestive of the spinning wheel.

Ex. 63 *Mädchenlied*

The first two verses are strophic, but in the third verse, by the simple means of two quaver rests in the melody indicative of the girl's broken voice, Brahms heightens her emotion, her sense of hopelessness. And in the final strophe, the masterstroke of all, at the despairing outcry "wofür soll ich spinnen?," the melody goes major and higher in pitch above off-beat, D♯-minor harmonies exacerbated at the "ich weiss es nicht" by a *sf*, lacerating, augmented triad. The final repetition of "ich weiss es nicht" to slow, descending crotchets accentuates the girl's grief like a sigh almost too painful for expression, and the four-bar postlude, falling wearily through two octaves, comes like a forlorn echo.

Ex. 64 *Mädchenlied*

The song is a masterpiece and every bit as poignant a piece of music and as moving a psychological study of a girl's desolation as Wolf's *Das verlassene Mägdlein*.

Returning to Op. 105, in the last three songs alone we are given a variety of style and mood that should forever silence those critics who prate about Brahms's limitations. Earlier in this study I singled out *Erinnerung, Abschied,* and *Über die See* as examples of Brahms's supreme melodic gift and his power to get to the heart of a poem's mood by melody alone, supported by the simplest of accompaniments. *Klage (III)* is the fourth and last instance of this, and no less moving. It is one of the comparatively few unvaried strophic songs, and on studying it one understands why. To begin with, the three verses of the poem (a folk text from Zuccalmaglio's *Deutsche Volkslieder mit ihren Originalweisen*) are in the same mood, so that no violation is done by their being set to the same melody. Then the melody itself is so charged with pathos, has such depths, that alone and unaided it is able to bear the weight of the lament that cries out against the frailty and treason of love—a love that has left the poet heartbroken in a world of winter-grief. The accompaniment, simple though it is, adds depth to depth. The song begins in F major but ends in the relative minor, and it is left to the postlude to persuade it gently back to the home key like some comforting friend. It is not only a little masterpiece in its own right but the final testimony of the lifelong influence of folk song on the master's art.

Auf dem Kirchhofe, the first of the two settings of Liliencron, opens with what is perhaps the most arresting prelude to be found in any of the songs. The first line of the poem, "Der Tag ging regenschwer und sturmbewegt," is dramatically anticipated in the upward-sweeping arpeggios and *f* chords, which seem to burst on the scene like the storm of the poem.

4. Auf dem Kirchhofe

Detlev von Liliencron

we‑sen,   verwittert Stein und Kreuz, die Krän‑ze alt,   die Namen ü‑ber‑

wachsen, kaum zu le‑sen.

Ex. 65 *Auf dem Kirchhofe*

The vocal line is more recitative than melody, as if the stroller were talking to himself as he looks at the grave stones and reads the inscriptions. The thunderous arpeggios and chords return for the second stanza, but then, following the climax at "Gewesen" and with the passing of the storm and gloomy thoughts, and looking towards the final "Genesen," the tempestuous C minor is replaced by a hushed C-major melody (a quotation from an old chorale), an inspired coda of tranquillity that comes like a windless sunset after a tempestuous day. And the final major chord of the postlude, so perfectly placed, sums up the voice's epilogue with a quiet radiance.

Verrat, like the earlier *Entführung,* is an attempt to compose in a style utterly unsuited to the composer's essentially lyrical genius. The minor Loewe did such things better. The song stands very much to Brahms as *Die beiden Grenadiere* does to Schumann and *Der Feuerreiter* to Wolf, in that they are essays in a style alien to the composer, and so synthetic. For all three composers, melodrama could only be factitious. *Ständchen* is an endearing, well-known song needing little commentary. It should be noted, however, that the simple charm of this moonlight nocturne, as Kalbeck very aptly called it,* conceals a vast amount of technical skill. The imitation of the students' flute, fiddle, and

*M. Kalbeck, *Johannes Brahms.*

zither in the accompaniment is infinitely deft, as is the counter-point hidden in it. And finally there is the magical transformation at the end from student gaiety to wistful tenderness, as the girl, hearing the serenade in half-sleep, murmurs her dreamy "Vergiss nich mein!"

Auf dem See (II), a setting of a poem by Reinhold depicting two lovers on a lake, lost to the world in their "floating Eden" as they glide over the water, is a barcarolle. It must be confessed that the rocking 6/8 melody, like Schubert's *Sie mir gegrüsst*, comes dangerously near to an overluscious sweetness, and in fact would have been open to that criticism but for the role played by the piano. Had Brahms given the song no more than a simple *arpeggiando* accompaniment with the strong beat falling re-morselessly on the first beat of the bar, it would have been no more than a voluptuous Viennese waltz. But instead we are given one of the most perfect examples of the all-important part an accompaniment can play in lifting the quality of a song, and a splendid example of Brahms's genius for just this. Instead of a monotonously regular 6/8 pulse, we meet with several diversi-ties: off-beat imitation and cross-rhythm.

Ex. 66 *Auf dem See (II)*

Formally, the song is yet another example of that amorphous hybrid between the varied strophic and through-composed that Brahms made his own. Phrases overlap, entwine, half repeat, and echo earlier phrases, yet move on in an infinitely varied way, continually recreating themselves. The modulations and cross-rhythms of the accompaniment reach their apotheosis in the last verse at "als ein schwimmend Eden trag es" (marked *immer ruhiger werdend*). But in this instance one may have some sympathy with Elisabeth von Herzogenberg, who complained of the passage to the composer as being too "bristly," too "full of harmonic obstacles" to be a satisfactory picture of a lover's paradise. Her objection is, I think, a valid one. The accompaniment here is too ingenious by half. Undoubtedly the instrumental composer took over here from the songwriter and, forgetful of the text, and seeing in the melodic line complex harmonic and rhythmic possibilities, treated it as he might have done an instrumental chamber work where it would have been completely irrefragable. Highly reprehensible, no doubt: but it does not detract more than fragmentarily from a song that is a bewitching illustration of the warmer, more winning, and more human side of the composer's nature.

In its piquant, deliberately insistent rhythm and ambiguous tonality, *Es hing der Reif* strongly anticipates the E-minor *Intermezzo* Op. 116, no. 5, and in doing so captures completely the mood and prosody of Groth's poem. The hoar frost whitens the linden tree, but the house of his beloved, all lighted and gay, and the vision of her at her window, glowing and warm, deludes him into imagining it is spring—until her cold greeting as she passes by forces him back to the realization that it is indeed still winter. The dreamlike quality of the poem is recreated to perfection in the mournful melody and the deliberately repetitive, almost sinister accompaniment with its falling bass line that sinks

deeper and deeper with the remorseless persistence of an incon-
solable grief.

Ex. 67 *Es hing der Reif*

The hint of sunshine in the middle section brings the warmer
key of A♭, harmonies, and a more resilient melody, but the
change is evanescent, and with the chill, loveless greeting the
atmosphere of frost and winter returns. The long-drawn arching
phrase of the voice on the final "Frost und Winter war," sung

above bare chords, so typically Brahms, comes like a cry of utter heartbreak.

Ex. 68 *Es hing der Reif*

Brahms gives only one directive—*Träumerisch*— and this must be kept in the forefront of the interpreters' minds when performing the song, for it is the key to its interpretation. The listener must be made to sense the dreamlike aura, or the magic is lost.

One can understand why the text of the next song, *Meine Lie-*

der, by Adolf Frey, appealed to Brahms. Its elusive text makes it all but untranslatable. It is a poet's reverie, saying nothing and everything. Those somber thoughts, that yearning after the unattainable, the striving after words that shall express them—where do they come from? The composer could feel in the poem the same mysterious vibrations that set in motion his own melodies. Frey's ponderings are made even more evanescent and at the same time more luminous and concentrated by the pensive melody and F#-minor harmonies. The nebulous passage at the words "und die Schatten von Cypressen," in which the vocal line repeats alternating D's while falling a semitone after each one above a pp harmony of uncertain dominant sevenths, is particularly expressive, as too is the final stanza, where the vocal line is emphasized and darkened by unisons in the accompaniment. The postlude, an extension of the prelude, sums up the song, its melody hovering semitonally above and below the pivotal C# like a bird trying to escape from a net, like the poet's thoughts struggling for expression. The song will never be one of the more popular ones, but for the Brahms devotee its pensive intimacy and lyrical beauty must give it a high place in his esteem.

The poem of *Ein Wanderer*, the last of Op. 106, in its theme is reminiscent of Schubert's *Der Wegweiser*. Like the Schubert/Müller wanderer, this later one of Brahms/Reinhold sees in the guidepost and the crossroads a visible sign of his tragic destiny. The road he must follow leads to that bourn from which no traveler returns. There and there only will he find his home and rest of spirit. The two songs have another factor in common: both are masterpieces. In this song of Brahms's, a splendid example of his varied-strophic form incidentally, the music is forward-driven like the wanderer himself as though by some relentless compulsion towards the final goal. At the "Keiner wird mich doch verstehen" of the second verse, and immediately following the music's sudden and unexpected veering into G♭ major, the right hand accompaniment, hitherto one of dark but smoothly running semiquavers, changes to a dotted rhythm expressive of the wanderer's febrile agitation, while along with it the bass descends in slow, heavy crotchets like some hypnotic force dragging him onward. The terse postlude, echoing the one-bar prelude, seems in its final two bars to sum up the whole song.

We now have only three songs left for consideration before coming to the ultimate Op. 121: *An die Stolze, Salamander*, and

Maienkätzchen. The first is deceptively easy on the ear, giving the impression on a first casual hearing of a not especially memorable melody flowing smoothly along above a typical interweaving accompaniment. Only with a closer study does its remarkably distinctive character become apparent. For it is, with the possible exception of *Auf dem Kirchhofe,* Brahms's nearest approach to Schumann and Wolf, in that the basic creative force behind the song is the piano (the harmony) with the melody superimposed. The pianist may well tell himself he is embarking on a solo Intermezzo. He will observe too that (1) on the repeat of the melody by the voice his own repeat is transferred from the right hand to the left under pedal E's and A's in the treble, and (2) for the second verse, while the vocal line is strophic, his own countermelody is, for the first half of it, placed an octave higher. Whether Brahms had been influenced here by Wolf, in spite of his antipathy, or whether the creation was purely a spontaneous redirecting of his attitude to the composition of lieder, we cannot know; but here it is for all the world to see, and yet another enduring testimony to his range and versatility. While technically the song is perfect, we are left with a slight unease and must pose a query as to the overriding aspect I stressed earlier, and one more important than technical perfection, namely—does the music interpret the mood, get to the heart, of the poem? Reactions to music vary, of course; but I personally am not happy that the bitter words of the poet addressed to "the haughty One" who scorns him are quite matched by the music. To me it seems a little too amiable, too smooth, in the final lines especially where he cries: "So dass ich zweifle fast, ob du ein Herze hast." This, one feels, should be given a musical equivalent of savage despair like that of Schubert's *Die Lieber hat gelogen* and *Du liebst mich nicht,* or Schumann's *Ich grolle nicht.* Nevertheless it is a fine song and to be recommended for serious consideration by lieder singers.

Wolf's attempts at humor in various songs, whatever their effect on Teutonic ears, can only cause mild embarrassment to English ones, reminding us that German humor is no laughing matter. That Brahms had a robust sense of humor is borne out by many of his remarks to friends about music, art, and life in general, and by songs like *Während des Regens, Des Liebsten Schwur, Unüberwindlich, Vergebliches Ständchen* and *Der Jäger*. However, one should not push the argument too far, such songs being the exception rather than the rule. So it is with dubious feelings that one notes the direction *mit Laune* (or *con humor*) at the nead of *Salamander*. Now, humor in ordinary life is a very delicate, complicated, and personal attribute; in music, as against literature, its successful attainment is rare indeed. Only Haydn reaches the heights of pure comedy, with Beethoven in second place. Brahms is too serious-minded to raise a laugh, so that when, as here, he deliberately makes the effort, the result, as with Wolf, is dismal. In addition to his own temperament, the text does nothing to help him. One can hardly raise a smile, let alone rock with hilarity, over a poem that relates how a salamander, thrown into the fire by a girl, says how delighted he is, and to which fable the poet adds the reflection: "That's just like me. I'm a cool devil, untouched by the fire of passion." The song might be about anything for all the atmosphere it engenders; and the best we can say about it is that its attempt at irony marks it out as a unique essay by Brahms in pure objectivity. The trouble is that such objectivity can all too easily produce no more than an unconvincing neutral art form, as it does here, the result being neither good Brahms nor good anything else.

The naive little poem that makes up *Maienkätzchen* could be ascribed to folk verse if one did not know that Liliencron was the author. Everything in Brahms—his empathy with folk song, his melodic gift, his harmonic and rhythmic genius, his sympathy with love in all its moods, his essential lyricism— leaped to meet the artless text. Nor did he make the mistake of endowing it with passion, with more emotion than it displays. For after all, what does it suggest? What is its mood? Sadness? Nostalgia? Pleasure? A shrug at the remembrance? Everything is left to the imagination. So, echoing the Volkslied simplicity of it, Brahms, gives us the ultimate proof of his lifelong spiritual affinity with folk song by creating an exquisite little miniature that is yet, like all his mature work, full of hidden subtleties. In the first two lines, for example, note the overlapping echo effect of the accompaniment.

Ex. 69 *Maienkätzchen*

and in the second verse (the song is through-composed), the introduction for the first time into the vocal line of the rhythmic phrase of the prelude at "einst brach ich euch."

Ex. 70 *Maienkätzchen*

Like Schumann's exquisite *Schneeglöckchen*, it is one of those songs whose very simplicity defies analysis and yet brings us close to tears. And moreover, in all probability it was the last song Brahms was to write for ten years.

7

Epilogue

Following the five songs of Op. 107, a silence in the realm of the Lied descended on Brahms—a silence that was to last for a decade, though a gap was filled by a series of instrumental masterpieces: the string quintet Op. 111, the clarinet chamber music, the Opp. 116–119 piano works, and the publication of his 49 *Deutsche Volkslieder* in 1894. In that decade he was to know the grief caused by the death of old friends, which is the lot of all who live to see their sixties. His former loves, Elizabeth von Herzogenberg and Hermine Spies; his contemporaries, Liszt, Tchaikovsky, and Wagner; and his close friend, Theodor Billroth, had all died. And in this year of 1896, four decades after their first momentous meeting, the shadow of his greatest love, Clara Schumann, was thrown yet again across his path. Her illness filled him with foreboding and dread. She was dying, and he knew it. It is no wonder, then, that the aging composer (he was now sixty-three—not old by our standards but considered advanced then—and showing signs of physical frailty), by nature melancholy and pessimistic, should find his thoughts turning more and more persistently towards the idea of death. Like Samuel Johnson, like many intellectuals, Brahms had a deep-seated secret dread of it. As an agnostic, he had no belief in a future existence. To him, death was the end of the road; the end not only of the ills of life but the joys as well—of the things that make this life worthwhile: nature, love, friendship, music, books, and art. To say goodbye to all that requires fortitude. Johnson tried to combat his fear by sporadic bursts of piety. Brahms, more honest with himself, felt he could do nothing but endure. In such cases, the creative artist will often strip his spirit bare through his art. Brahms had done this in many of his songs, and his last piano and chamber works are tinged with valediction. Their time of year is autumnal, of day, of sunset— beautiful but infinitely sad, presaging winter and night.

It was now, in the May of 1896, that, surprising his remaining friends who believed he had put songwriting behind him, he brought out the *Vier ernste Gesänge*. One understands at once, with the biographical facts in mind, why he chose to set these Biblical texts at this time. The stoical pessimism and abnegation of *Ecclesiastes* and *Ecclesiasticus* expressed his feelings about life and death with a perfection he had never found before. Through them, inspiration returned to enable him to compose his final farewell both to his own life and that of his beloved Clara.* He was only too well aware of the effect they would have on the pious, and he made feeble attempts to minimize the shock by sallies of typically crusty humor in his letters and conversation. "I have given myself a birthday present," he said to Max Kalbeck on 7 May 1896, as he showed him the manuscript. To his publisher, Simrock, he wrote next day: "I have amused myself on my birthday by writing a few little songs." And later he asked his friend Dr. Ophüls if public performance of such "altogether godless songs" could be prohibited on religious grounds; while in a letter to Heinrich von Herzogenberg he expressed unease in case they might lay him open to attack for "un-Christian opinions."** We can smile at those fears today, but the religious atmosphere of the last century made them very real.

To come to the songs themselves. The fact that they were his last and in fact his penultimate opus,*** that he died the following April, and that they are settings of biblical words and may be said to represent his ultimate contribution to nineteenth-century music, have caused generations of commentators to surround them with an almost sacred aura. "The crown of his life's work," "the apotheosis of nineteenth-century lieder," and similar phrases are commonplace in program notes. They have become to Brahms, in fact, much as the late quartets to Beethoven—a

*She died 20 May 1896, two weeks after the composition of the songs.
**Friedländer, *Brahms's Lieder.*
***His last published work was the *Eleven Choral Preludes* Op. 122.

sort of temple where before worshipping one must take off one's shoes and enter with closed eyes and holy dread. Now, it is true that these works do represent the consummation of their respective composer's achievements. At the same time it appears to me that the warning notice put outside their confines by so many admirers to the effect that the newcomer is about to enter strange and sacred territory and may get lost in bewildering labyrinths is officious and unnecessary. No intelligent musical person who has studied Beethoven right from his beginnings and through his so-called "three periods," giving special attention to the last cello sonatas, bagatelles, piano sonatas, and variations, will have difficulty when it comes to the last quartets, for it will be found that, though different in some aspects, fundamentally they grow out of the preceding works. Similarly with these *Vier ernste Gesänge*. No one who has taken the trouble to study the lieder from Op. 3 to Op. 107 will have difficulty in coming to terms with Op. 121. What he will find is that they are conceived differently from the rest. Gone is the marvelously fluid line. In its place we find a quasi-declamatory style for the voice, with an accompaniment seeming at times like a piano reduction of an orchestral score.* But if different technically, in their somber poignancy, dark tone color, and despairing character they are simply a follow-up to the Requiem. The stark acceptance of death as the enemy of life, expressed in the harrowing words of the old writers of Ecclesiastes and Ecclesiasticus, extend the humanistic philosophy of the Requiem, but now expressed in a more personal and relentless way.

The introductory bars of the first song—(*Denn es geht dem Menschen*)—with its bleak opening fifths and octaves, is reminiscent of the *Requiem*, not only thematically but in its fatalistic reflection on life and death. It is the musical equivalent, in fact, of the Preacher's *All is Vanity*.

*Brahms in fact began sketching an orchestral version but never completed it.

Ex. 72 *Ich wandte mich*

The unexpected *allegro* at "Es fahrt alles an einen Ort" over the piano's scurrying quaver triplets is an outcry of despair, breaking down the pristine stoicism. The iron control of the *andante* returns briefly, only to be swept aside again by the frenetic *allegro*, which, after dying away on the query "was nach ihm geschehen wird?" is pulled up and dismissed in two clenching D-minor chords.

The second song—*Ich wandte mich*—is the shortest and most concentrated of the four, and opens oppressively with those falling G-minor octaves to which I have already referred.*

Ex. 71 *Denn es geht dem Menschen*

Their expression of hopelessness is even intensified by the closing passage in the major—a cry of utter heartbreak.

*See p. 50.

Ex. 73 Ich wandte mich

But it is the third song, again beginning minor and ending major—*O Tod, wie bitter bist du*—that forms the emotive climax of the work. This direct apostrophe to death first as enemy and then as friend is one of the most harrowing expressions of the human spirit ever penned.

Ex. 74 *O Tod, wie bitter bist du*

Yet again, it is in the closing episode in the major that Brahms touches the highest peak of all.

Ex. 75 *O Tod, wie bitter bist du*

The last song, a setting of St. Paul's discourse on charity, or love (dependent on which translation of his agape one accepts, and yet again on one's interpretation of love) is a revocation of the previous despairing trinity, a *volte face* from their fatalism to a desperate attempt at hopefulness. And coming as it does immediately after one of the most searing pieces of music ever written, the first half of it at least, with its near-jaunty rhythm that does not suit the words anyway, can only be felt as an anticlimax, a shrug of forced optimism much like the finale of Beethoven's Choral symphony after the brooding *adagio molto*. Only with the radiant B-major *adagio* episode and the final return to the tonic major key of the *sostenuto* coda (Example 76) does the music rise to the heights of the preceding songs, then indeed leaving us on a pinnacle of inspiration.

Ex. 76 *Wenn ich mit Menschen-und mit Eengelzunken redete*

Brahms himself, Geiringer tells us, could not bear to hear the songs performed for fear of being moved too deeply, and one can understand that well enough. Too poignant to be sung in public, they are, at least it seems to me, a secret lament for the private ear and heart.*

Much has been written about these songs, but nothing more

---

*Especially if, like the present writer, one has the good fortune to possess the Ferrier recording of the work. The knowledge, added to the power of the music, that she too was so soon to die, intensifies the emotion beyond bearing.

cogently descriptive than the words of Engelmann in a letter to the composer soon after their publication, in which he commentated on their "lapidary simplicity."* They are indeed as if hewn from stone, to stand like four granite pillars in a vast arena— stern, implacable, timeless, inviolable. With this opus, one feels, Brahms was taking his farewell of life, and recognizes in it the truth of the Latin tag *Finis coronat opus*. For Brahms, the end surely crowned the lifework.

With the *Four Serious Songs* we take leave not only of Brahms but of nineteenth-century lieder. The German lied is an achievement equaled only by the sonata principle innovated and perfected by the great Viennese classical composers. Of that achievement the songs of Brahms, no less than those of Wolf, are a crowning consummation.

*Friedländer, *Brahms's Lieder.*

8

Songs for More than One Voice with Piano

Duets: Opp. 20, 28, 61, 66, 75

Coming to the songs for more than one voice, we leave the world of the professional recitalist for that of the amateur, to enjoy the "social" music-making beloved of Schubert and his friends. Composed for group performance rather than being inspired like the lieder by a poem and a mood, it is not surprising that, viewed as a whole, they do not attain the heights of the solo songs. Yet to a great composer, and especially to one as self-critical as Brahms, such a challenge would not be accepted lightly. And in fact among these chamber works, which, incidentally, cover almost the whole of the composer's creative life, are to be found examples comparable to the great lieder.

Of the three Op. 20 songs for soprano and alto, the two *Weg der Liebe* are settings of the Herder translation of our well-known seventeenth-century anonymous poem *Love will find out the way*, and, while melodiously attractive, are unadventurous and fail altogether to catch the bravado spirit of the verses as the English folk melody does. For the third number, *Das Meere*, a translation of an Italian text in which the deeps of the ocean and those of love are compared, Brahms has set a lilting rhythm in 6/8 meter, a melody harmonized in ingratiating Mendelssohnian thirds and sixths, and a simple barcarolle accompaniment—attractive if lightweight.

With the four Op. 28 songs for alto and baritone we regain the solo heights. The first, *Die Nonne und der Ritter*, dedicated to Amalie Joachim, is a setting of Eichendorff so romantically vague as almost to defy interpretation. The nun, looking out from her cell window, her longing "awake with the stars," recalls memories of the knight, while he, similarly thinking of her, decides to go and fight and perhaps die in the Crusade. Nothing is explained: all is veiled and suggested. Such a poem manifestly appealed to Brahms, for whom the themes of fatal love and death were almost obsessive. The construction of the duet is unusual, consisting mostly as it does of antiphonal solos by the two protagonists, with very little ensemble. It opens with a slow, sombre eighteen-bar solo for the alto voice (the Nun) with only static chords for accompaniment.

Ex. 77 *Die Nonne und der Ritter*

Following a seven-bar interlude for the piano, the baritone (the Knight) takes over and sings the same theme in the relative major with a slightly different piano bass. After a second piano interlude of ten bars, the Nun repeats her lugubrious melody, now harmonized by a less-static accompaniment suggestive of increasing agitation. After eight bars from the piano, the baritone repeats the melody; but now the accompaniment becomes fuller and more urgent, and after twelve bars of it the voices come together for the first time, but even then for only four bars, when the alto resumes her solo for sixteen bars, at which point, above a now-febrile accompaniment of *tremolos* and abrupt *forte* interjections the baritone takes over for sixteen bars until the two voices combine for an impassioned climax. But even here the duetto is brief, and the song concludes as it began, with the Nun's dirge-like melody fading into exhausted silence completed by a piano coda ending, ironically, major. The song is one of the most deeply felt and original in all Brahms, and repays endless study.

The second song, *Vor der Tür*, is a needed contrast. Brahms must have jumped at the opportunity offered by the folk text, the theme being the same as the one that was to inspired him some twenty years later with one of his best-known lieder, namely, the *Vergebliches Ständchen*. As in the solo song, the impetuous lover implores his sweetheart to let him in, only to be refused and summarily dismissed. The lover begins his entreaty solo; the girl replies with the same melody. But whereas in the solo song the two voices never combine, here the song now becomes a duet, the voices blending and contrasting in mood, he all bluster and demand, she head-tossing and adamant; while throughout, the accompaniment is vintage Brahms, varied from verse to verse, and a joy for the pianist (though a tricky one if the *vivace* and *sotto voce* are to be brought off).

Among the nearly two hundred solo songs only five are settings of Goethe, not one of which can be placed among the composer's greatest. With the third of thee duets, *Es rauschet das Wasser*, the composer made amends to the poet, for it is one of the most beautiful and haunting. The love theme, similar to that in the great *Von ewiger Liebe*, would naturally endear itself to Brahms. Following the exquisite prelude, the alto voice enters, declaring in a long-phrased typical melody that like the waters on the earth and the stars in the heavens, human love is mutable;

to which the baritone replies in an equally transcendent melody that unlike those mutables true love is constant. For the rest of the song, in a miraculous sleight-of-hand wizardry, Brahms combines the two melodies, but varying the climax and leaving the male voice to finish solo in a consolatory assertion of faith. The song ends with a postlude which that the prelude, with two bars added to bring the music to a full close in the home key. The song is a masterpiece in miniature, and as such I quote it unreservedly in full.

Ex. 78 *Es rauschet das Wasser*

Der Jäger und sein Liebchen forms a splendid finale to the set,
its impetuous headlong *allegro* indicative of the young huntsman's desire to meet his beloved, making it something of a *tour
de force* guaranteed to bring down the house.

Against these Op. 28 duos, those of Opp. 61, 66, and 75, with
one or two exceptions, can only be described as average Brahms.
Phänomen is the best of Op. 61, and is a setting of Goethe taken
from his *West-Oestlicher Divan*, with the poet at his most per-
versely epigrammatic, seeing in nature's phenomenon of the
rainbow a symbol of hope and love even for old age. The music
is rich in Brahmsian fingerprints: the B-major key with melody
and accompaniment reminiscent of the opening bars of the Op.
8 piano trio.

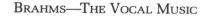

Ex. 79 *Phänomen*

Its construction is simple ABA. In the B section the music becomes canonic, from which it makes its effortless return to A via the dominant key of F♯ major.

The text of *Am Strande*, the outstanding number of Op. 66, is by Hölty. The gentle plash and murmur of the waves, says the poet, bring nostalgic memories, memories seemingly subsumed in the waves. The merest glance at the first page, with its typical cross-rhythm piano prelude, tells us that Brahms intends to make something out of the poem.

Ex. 80 *Am Strande*

Again the structure is ternary. In the middle episode, note the unexpected G♭/C♭ modulations, all leading back magically to the home key of E♭.

The only other numbers of these opera worth mentioning are *Edward* and *Walpurgisnacht*, the first and last of the Op. 75 4 *Ballads and Romances*. The former, for alto and tenor, is a setting of the well-known Scottish ballad. While one may concede to it a certain dark power, it does not match up to Loewe's dramatic version. This Brahms setting, for two sopranos, consists of a dialogue between a mother and daughter, which the composer must have set with tongue in cheek, and which Elisabeth von Herzogenberg described in a letter to the composer as a "shuddery witches' duet."* The A minor, 6/8 *presto* of the accompaniment, suggesting the witches' broomstick ride, the clashing harmonies, and the "shuddery" atmosphere, all lead to the girl's horrified realization that her mother is herself one of the witches.

Quartets: Opp. 31, 64, 92, 103, 112, 52, 65

Taken as a whole, the quartets attain a higher level of achievement than the duets, while the best of them could be accepted as stepping straight out of the *Liebeslieder Waltzer*, to which no higher accolade can be awarded. The text of the first of Opus 31, *Wechsellied zum Tanze*, though by Goethe, is nothing more than a good-natured skirmish of words between two disparate pairs of dancers—the dispassionate ones who dance for the mere joy of dancing, (*Die Gleichgultigen*), and the tender-hearted (*Die*

*Friedländer, *Brahms's Lieder.*

Zärtlichen) who demand a love-partner. Brahms sets the duo-logue as an antiphon, with the former represented by the altos and basses, the latter by the sopranos and tenors. The *Gleichgultigen* lead off to a C-minor minuet rhythm.

1. Wechsellied zum Tanze
Goethe

Ex. 81 *Gleichgultigen*

to be followed (after a modulation into A♭ by the *Zärtlichen*) with this melody.

Ex. 82 Zärtlichen

Both pairs repeat their protestations similarly; but for the conclusion they combine, the former singing their theme in the minor, the latter in the major, while the wonderful accompaniment takes them through Schubertian enharmonic modulations to the end. The song, though nothing more than a lighthearted dalliance, through the alchemy of genius is transmuted into a work that anticipates the *Liebeslieder*.

The text of the next song *(Neckereien)* is also a spate of love verbiage, as its title (meaning "banter") proclaims, between HE and SHE. The male voices begin in canon; the female voices retort in homophony; the males take over the female melody as if in mockery; then the voices combine *animato*, becoming more and more forceful and excited, gyrating round one another in growing complexity until the males, as though exhausted, slow down to a resigned *p*, only to be galvanized by the sudden *f* entrance of the females for the last two bars. All through, the piano accompaniment is sheer Brahms, subtle and independent. It is all superb musical fooling and lightheartedness, but with hidden depths.

Der Gang zum Liebchen is the first of the two settings made by Brahms of this Bohemian folk text, the second being the solo song Op. 48, no. 1. On first coming to this quartet version, the listener will be startled at hearing a familiar melody, due to the fact that Brahms used it again for the better known E-major Waltz, Op. 39, no. 5, for piano duet. It should be remarked, though, that here the accompaniment is altogether different, and with a beautiful coda added.

With the three quartets of Op. 64, we jump ten years. The first *(An die Heimat)* might well stand as a perfect example of the alleged overlushness brought against the composer by the anti-Brahms faction. *Schmalz*, it must be conceded, is abundant here. One feels that the word *Heimat* has evoked a too-emotional response—too emotional and too prolonged, at least to British ears, German reaction being what it may.

Der Abend, marked *rühig*, perfectly catches the sense of peace invoked by the text, despite Schiller's prevalence for complicating his scenery with classical allusions--a factor that gave Schubert difficulty with his settings of the poet. The song is the simplest and most restrained of these quartets, its highlight being the exquisite piano accompaniment rather than the vocal setting.

With the last of the set, Brahms returns to his favorite poet, Daumer, whose love effusions were to provide him with more songs than those of any other poet. *Fragen* (Questions) is typical Daumer verse. The poet, inevitably lovesick, flings questions to his tormented heart: Why are you so sad, so torn with longing? Why can't you forget her and return to quiet days and sleep of nights? To which the Heart replies, as expected, that to forget her and know peace of mind again is impossible. Brahms sets the Daumer text to a folksong-like melody in a lilting 6/8 A major, with a lovely modulation into F major for the central episode, the male and female voices sometimes alternating, sometimes together, all superbly harmonized, with a completely independent accompaniment suggestive of the lover's agitated yearnings.

Another leap of a decade brings us to the four quartets of Op. 92, and in each of these we find fulfilled the later Brahms, nostalgic, introspective, complex, and original. The very first song, *O schöne Nacht*, seems to shimmer with the poet's nocturnal picture of moonlight, the nightingale, and the agitated, breathless expectation of the lover as he hurries to his meeting with his beloved. All the Brahms fingerprints are here: the atmospheric prelude with its softly rising E-major *arpeggios* and syncopated thirds; the harmonic richness; the cross-rhythms in the accompaniment. One is tempted to quote the whole of this masterpiece in miniature, but I content myself with a snippet from the fervent interjacence of the lover to the closing bars, with their subtle reminiscence of the prelude leading miraculously to the final benediction on a repeat of the opening words "O schöne Nacht."

Ex. 83 *O schöne Nacht*

Spätherbst is a complete contrast. The poet, Hermann Allmers, was later to inspire Brahms with *Feldeinsamkeit,* one of his greatest and best-known lieder; and just as that was a tone poem of summer, so this is one of autumn, with a picture of dripping mist, grey skies, songless birds, and leafless trees distressing the human heart. The song is the shortest and most intense of the set, and in its gray, E-minor key, its repetitive staccato piano trip-lets, and its strophic form for the two verses, it suggests the ceaseless drip of the clinging mist and the stark gloom of the scene.

With *Abendlied,* yet another change of mood. The poem speaks of a sense of peace and release coming to the heart with the quiet close of day, making life seem like a slumber song. The score is the simplest of the set in texture and is perhaps the least success-ful in catching the atmosphere of the poem.

With *Warum?* Goethe again. He asks: Why do songs soar heaven-ward? Shouldn't they rather bring the stars, moon, and sun down to us? It is difficult to understand what sort of mood such a poem might evoke from a composer. Brahms keeps a somewhat neutral one. The most original and startling moment in the song is the prelude, which, after leaping upward on powerful f, F_7 chords, ends abruptly on the chord of $G\flat$, forcing the voices to enter in that key.

Ex. 84 *Warum?*

The *Zigeunerlieder* (Op. 103) form a curious collection. Originally, Brahms set eleven of these Hungarian folk texts (translated
into the German for him by Hugo Conrat) as SATB quartets with
piano accompaniment. This done, he then, in what appears to
have been an attempt to emulate with them the success he had
achieved for the piano with the Hungarian Dances, reset eight of
them for solo voice. The overall result, to the present writer at
least, is one of Brahms's less successful ventures; and he finds
himself in agreement with Elizabeth v. Herzogenberg, to whom
the composer sent manuscript copies when she confessed to the
opinion that the songs were neither genuine gypsy, Hungarian,
nor Brahms. Ironically, the outstanding song of the set is the
most intrinsically German, number 7, *Kommt dir manchmal in
den Sinn*—genuine Brahms in its melodic beauty and warm
harmonies.

Finally, the two Op. 112 quartets, and with these we recognize
the master lieder composer of the last phase and of such songs
as *Der Tod, das ist die kühle Nacht; Nachtigall; Immer leise wird
mein Schlummer;* and *Ein Wanderer,* with their overwhelming
sadness and autumnal nostalgia conveyed effortlessly with unsurpassed technical mastery. The very title of the first work—
Sehnsucht—proclaims the sort of music it will be. Poem and
music are among the saddest known expressions of human emotion. The F-minor prelude, the entry of the sopranos and altos

in melancholy thirds, followed similarly by the tenors and basses, the wonderful harmonies and modulations, the interweaving of the voices, the dying fall of the final bars on a diminished fifth collapsing as though in sheer exhaustion from pain into the embrace of the closing major chord—all these points are too poignant to be analyzed. One can only marvel and find this lament on human life too despairing for words. And as such I quote it in full.

Ex. 85 Sensucht

The second song, *Nächtens*, by the same poet, marks Brahms's farewell to the genre. If not so intense and searing as the first, both poem and music are nonetheless tragic. This nostalgic setting of Brahms has been unimprovably described by Peter Rummenhöller on the sleeve of the splendid recording of these works by the Kammerchor Stuttgart under Frieder Bernius (Intercord Klassiche Diskottlhel 130.809), and as such I quote: "*Nachtens*

... is not only a worthy close to the set, but also a signpost into the future. The strange, restless 5/4 meter and the continuous, quasi-impressionistic piano *tremolos* exalt the piece above every convention which originally governed this kind of social music." After which my only comment will be that one should note how the desolating D-minor prelude.

Ex. 86 *Nächtens*

is used to link the two verses and to close the work with its ironic major chord.

Ex. 87 *Nächtens*

No survey of the piano-accompanied vocal quartet could end without a reference to the two supreme examples of the genre that have achieved a modicum of popularity: the *Liebeslieder*

Waltzer (Op. 52) and its companion, the Neue Liebeslieder Waltzer (Op. 65). While none of the individual numbers may be greater than the quartets already noted, judged as a whole they stand as the ne plus ultra of them and, along with the Waltzer and Hungarian Dances for piano, as the unsurpassed expression not only of a rare, unbuttoned Brahms but an unrivaled Brahms.

These Waltzer, in fact, standing midway in the composer's development, are the offshoot of several facets of his life. To begin with, Daumer's poems, despite their being only feeble imitations of Goethe's Westöstlicher Divan, nevertheless appealed to Brahms just as his other indifferent poems had done.

Then other influences undoubtedly came into play: the composer's new-found love for Vienna, now his permanent home; a sense of relief and new hope once he had put behind him his grief on the death of his mother and the nerve-racking composition of the Requiem; and finally the sudden unfulfilled emotional entanglement he had come to experience with Clara Schumann's daughter Julie—a passion that remained secret and untold but, when he learned of her engagement made him, according to Clara herself, "a changed man." It was while he was in the throes of his new love that he wrote the Liebeslieder Waltzer, and after the loss of her, the tragic Alto Rhapsody.

To come to the music itself. The two sets comprise thirty-three loosely-strung Viennese waltzes* bound together only by the theme of love in all its moods: passion, tenderness, anger, jealousy, reproach, and confession ad finem, yet so subtly linked by a sense of continuity as to give the impression of a song cycle. Astonishingly, the all-important vocal part was printed as ad lib by Simrock with the idea of repeating the success of the Op. 39 pianoforte duet Waltzer by making it attractive to pianists and so financially more viable. But Brahms put his foot down, writing protestingly to the publisher, "The Waltzes must appear just as they stand. Whoever wishes to play them without the voice will have to do so from the full score. Under no circumstances may they be published without the voice parts. This is how they must

---

*The one exception is the final. "Zum Schluss" of the Neue Liebeslieder, which is structurally a passacaglia with a 9/4 time signature. The reason for this was probably because while the text for the rest was taken from Daumer's Polydora, for this "coda" to the set, Brahms went to Goethe, whose poem expresses more profound sentiments.

be brought before the public. And let us hope they will become real family music, and sung a lot."*

The composer's wishes were fulfilled. And so popular did the first set become that he felt called on to compose a second: hence the *Neue Liebeslieder* of five years later. Unlike so many "sequels," the later set shows no loss of inspiration in comparison with the earlier one. On the contrary, if choice had to be made, the Op. 65 might reasonably claim to be the richer in its piano part and its harmonic coloring. But such comparisons are odious and unnecessary, both being gems from the master's workshop. And one can easily understand why these enchanting works were taken spontaneously to the musical public's heart. To hear them, and even more, to take part in them, is to be bewitched by them forever. Each of the numbers is a masterpiece in miniature, melodically, harmonically, and rhythmically. And so subtle is their rhythmic variety that one never feels any sense of monotony. Familiarity with these and the Op. 39 piano-duet waltzer might tempt anyone to believe that Brahms rather than Strauss should be regarded as "King of the Waltz."

After these masterworks the few remaining examples in this genre,—the four Zigeunerlieder (Op. 112), the drinking Glee *Tafellied* (Op. 93b) and the *Kleine Rochzietkantate*—are forgettable.

*Geiringer, *Brahms: His Life and Work.*

9

The Minor Choral Works

Study of these works provokes astonishment that Brahms, the reverse of Schubert here, while producing instrumental masterpieces, was groping and tentative with his coeval vocal ensembles. To give chapter and verse: while turning out the various psalms, motets, etc. for his Detmold and Hamburg choirs and even later, he was unleashing works like the Op. 18 Sextet, the D-minor piano concerto, the Schumann Variations, and the first two piano quartets. It is a strange dichotomy that I have examined and tried to explain at the end of this chapter, following a review of the works in question. Moreover it was an anomaly that applies not merely to the early compositions but right up to the very last.

For the moment, before looking at the titles involved, it must be noted that most of them are settings of scriptural and even liturgical texts, a fact so strange in itself in view of Brahms's known agnosticism as to enforce a brief look at the composer's background and temperament.

Although brought up in a North German Protestant religion and tradition, by middle age Brahms had lost his belief and never attended church. ("He believes in nothing!" the horror-struck, pious Dvořák exclaimed after a meeting with Brahms.) Nevertheless, that same upbringing with its basis in the Bible clung to him like a burr, as childhood and adolescent influences invariably do; so that although the Word ceased to have any religious meaning for him, loving literature and especially poetry as he did, the poetic and dramatic aspects of the Bible kept a lifelong fascination for him, and he turned to them for inspiration again and again.

But it is precisely here that the question of inspiration arises. Rossini boasted that he could set a laundry list to music. Well and good; but what sort of music would it be? No doubt he could have made a brilliant aria out of it, but one could have doubts as to its puristic worth. Similarly, an agnostic composer may set a religious text and make it musically acceptable; and if he is by gift and nature a dramatic composer, by carefully choosing his text he may even give us a masterpiece, as witness Verdi with his *Requiem*. But Brahms falls between the two schools of the sacred and the dramatic, the church and the theatre. Unable to accept Christian dogma or belief, he could not find inspiration in the liturgy of the Mass or the so-called "divinely inspired revelations" of the Bible, nor capture in musical terms the more dramatic narratives, being the subjective, introspective composer he essentially was. Thus there was no way he could summon the inspirational fervor of belief that inspired *The Messiah*, the *Passions* of Bach, the *Masses* of Haydn, the *Requiem* of Fauré, or the sense of theater that made the *Requiem* of Verdi possible and, to some degree, the *Masses* of Mozart.

Only in one from the many biblical texts he was to set was Brahms able to solve his own personal problem and produce a masterpiece. To leave the general for the particular, let us glance at these works, basing our comments on the Orwellian theory of equality in that, while almost all of them are minor productions, some are more minor than others. In published chronological order they are as follows:

Ave Maria (Op. 12). Composed in 1858 for his Hamburg Ladies' Choir, with accompaniment for organ or orchestra, and scored for SSAA. Based on the Latin text of the Catholic liturgy, the setting consists of only 101 bars, and in its austere simplicity reflects Brahms's study of sixteenth-century polyphonic church music to the extent of being completely impersonal. One wonders why the North German Protestant composer came to set it.

Begräbnissgesang (Burial Song) (Op. 13). Although composed at the same time as the preceding opus, the fact that instead of the casual *ad hoc* accompaniment for the work Brahms provides the Funeral Hymn for SATB chorus with a carefully-organized orchestral background of wind, brass, and timpani with strings deliberately omitted, and also that the text is in his native German (albeit semi-religious, sixteenth-century), all helped him to produce a work of some originality in which prophetic anticipation of later works, especially the *Requiem*, can be heard. While it can only be considered apprentice work as against his mature, major masterpieces, in its achievement of special tonal effects it shows evidence of that musical imagination, that secret gift of the inner ear, that stamps the true composer, and without which no creation of great orchestral or choral works is possible.

4 *Songs for Women's Voices* (Op. 17). The four texts* are strangely miscellaneous, and even more strangely scored for two horns and harp, the latter instrument obviously suggested by the first line of the Ruperti poem "Es tönt ein voller Harfen-clang." Here the composer is experimenting in tonal color. But again, musically the result is mediocre, the settings being simple to the point of naiveté, that of the Shakespeare (Feste's song, "Come away, come away, Death" in *Twelfth Night*) being particularly inept. The best is the Ossian, in which something of the somber Nordic, atmospheric verse is caught.

7 *Marienlieder* (Op. 22)* For SATB *a cappella* choir, and the composer's first work for unaccompanied part-song. More even than the rest of these smaller choral works, this opus, consisting of seven folk texts relating traditional legends of the Virgin Mary, reflects Brahms's saturation in the medieval church style: to such an extent indeed that a betting man would take 100–1 odds against anyone hearing them for the first time ascribing them to any post-sixteenth-century composer, let alone to Brahms. So archaic is their style, in fact, that they could be taken for traditional German carols arranged by Brahms himself. The composer probably realized this when he spoke of them as being "in the manner of old German church music and folk song."

Psalm XIII (Op. 27) For three-part women's voices (SSA) in three movement, with organ or piano accompaniment.

2 *Motets* (Op. 29) For SATBB *a cappella* choir,* text from Paul Speratus (sixteenth century).

Geistliches Lied (Op. 30) for SATB choir with organ or piano *ad lib.** Text by Paul Fleming (seventeenth-century).

3 Geistliche Chöre (Op. 37), for SSAA *a cappella* choir.*

---

*See Appendix for titles.

All the above works reveal two factors: (1) the advance made by the young composer in the techniques of composition and (2) the too-blatant influence of the St. Thomas Kirche cantor. In the Op. 29 especially, one finds mastery of every compositional technique: fugue, double canon, canon in unison, contrary motion, and close imitation—everything in fact except the characteristic that really counts, namely the stamp of the composer's own individuality.

Pursuing these smaller choral compositions through the 1860s and 1870s, and with the splendid solo songs of Opp. 43–72 behind him, one would have imagined Brahms would now be able to transmute the alchemy of his mature personality into any vocal ensembles. But remarkably such is not the case. The *Liebeslieder* apart, we find him still swimming in the archaic sea, or, as if in desperation to get out of it, in imitative folk-song vein. This may be said of the 5 *Songs for 4-part a cappella Men's Choir* Op. 41, *Songs for 6-Part a capella mixed Choir* Op. 42, *12 Songs & Romances for Women's Choir* Op. 44, *7 Songs for a cappella Mixed Choir* Op. 62, *Two Motets for a cappella Mixed Choir* Op. 74, and 6 *Songs & Romances for a cappella Mixed choir* Op. 93a.

The few exceptions to this general criticism are the *Vineta* (Op. 42) and the 5 *Songs for four-to-six-Part Choir and Piano* (Op. 104). And the reason why these numbers shine out like lonely planets from a skyful of faint stars is undoubtedly the texts. The former consists of a poem by Wilhelm Müller of Schubert *Die Schöne Müllerin* fame based on the legend of Vineta, a town that once stood on the mouth of the Oder but which, after being laid waste by the Danes in 1172, was submerged by the sea. But, legend goes on to say, its ruins are still to be seen deep under the waves and its bell towers heard faintly pealing.

> Aus des Meeres tiefem, tiefem Grunde
> Klingen Abendglocken, dumpf and matt.
> Uns zu geben wunderbare Kunde
> Von der schönen, alten Wunderstadt.*

The rhythm and substance of the verse are obviously inspirational to a composer, and when in addition the poet links the

---

*Prose translation: "From the depths of the sea faint sounds as though from tolling bells arise, telling of the existence of the submerged old town."

myth to himself with the final stanza,*

> Aus des Herzens tiefem, tiefem Grunde
> Klingt es mir wie Glocken, dumpf und matt
> Ach, sie geben wunderbare Kunde
> Von der Liebe, die geliebt es hat.

one can visualize Brahms chortling in his joy at finding a theme so dear to his heart.

The descriptive first verse engenders a ravishing melody with a lilting barcarolle rhythm cast in subtle five-bar phrasing.

Ex. 88 *Vineta*

*"And from the depths of my heart, too, soft sounds are swelling, telling of love so young and yet so old."

The middle section opens with a melismatic descent of octaves expressive of the poet's *Aus des Hezens tiefem, tiefem Grunde*, thereafter pursuing its way through a series of rich modulations until, after a pause on a diminished seventh, the song returns to and closes with a repeat of the first section.

After this genuine Brahms emanation, the rest of the Opus, apart from the 5 *Songs for a cappella mixed Choir* (Op. 104), are expendable. And the reason for these being exceptional is the same, namely, the texts; for they are from Rückert, Kalbeck, and Groth, favorite poets of Brahms, and redolent of nostalgia, a sense of farewell, of the end of things—sentiments and emotions that had always drawn the best from his inherent melancholy nature. The two Rückert nocturnes especially are true Brahms, ethereal and haunting.

The listener can only reflect with astonishment on the fact that over the span of some twenty years, when the foregoing, characterless vocal numbers were composed, Brahms had written such instrumental masterworks as the Piano Quartets Opp. 25 and 26, the "Handel" and "Paganini" Variations, the Piano Quintet, and the Horn Trio.

There remain Op. 109 and Op. 110. The three anthems that comprise the former, entitled *Fest- und Gedenksprüche*, were composed in 1889 as a gesture of thanks by the composer in return for receiving the freedom of Hamburg in that year. As a letter to his beloved Clara reveals, Brahms was deeply moved by this tribute (even if belated) from his native city, and expressed his intention of writing a choral work to celebrate the occasion. Written for eight-part a cappella mixed choir, the work is based on biblical texts carefully selected by the composer, and may be described as a patriotic cantata. But as commentators have not failed to note, Brahms has here committed an atrocious solecism. Ardent patriot that he was, and an admirer of Bismarck and his policy of war with France and of enforcing the unification of Germany under the aegis of its Emperor Wilhelm I, he chose part of the text with the Iron Chancellor in mind, oblivious of or indifferent to the fact that the St. Luke passage has Satan for its reference!*

---

*"When a strong man armed keepeth his palace, his goods are in peace. But when a stronger than he cometh . . . he taketh from him all his armour wherein he trusted and divideth the spoils."

Although a splendid exemplar of the composer's contrapuntal powers, and as such a joy for any choir to sing, by no stretch of the imagination can it be described as characteristic Brahms, and least of all as bearing out Hans Gal's hyperbolic estimation as "deserving a place among the most important *a cappella* compositions of all time,"* being as it is an aberrant juxtaposition of old and new elements, of *stile antico* and *stile moderno*, the archaic and the contemporary, with passages of average hymnody jostling others of piquant late-Brahms harmony.

With the *3 Motets* of Op. 110, Brahms made his final contribution to church music, using the same forces as the previous work. But although still liturgical, the text is very different in meaning, being personal to the composer and, like the *Requiem*, expressive of his desperate searching for consolation. "But I am afflicted and sorrowful, O Lord of abundant goodness and truth; look on me" runs the text of the first anthem, set for double choir. Beginning in E minor it closes in the relative major. The second anthem ("Thou poor vain world") is in F minor and for single choir, but, expressing the words "Grant me peace," ends on a major chord. With the third anthem the double chorus returns to begin in C minor antiphonally for "When we do suffer sore despair," but again ends in the major on a note of resignation. The work is really a replica of the previous one, seeking to express old texts to sixteenth- and seventeenth-century modes mixed with modern interpolations, making it neither purely archaic nor contemporary. Yet only six years later, with the Op. 121, Brahms was able to fuse biblical texts with his own genuine style and achieve a life-crowning masterpiece.

"Everything that passed Brahms's severe self-criticism deserves serious attention" is an asseveration made by more than one critic on the composer's output. Certainly, of all the great composers Brahms was the most self-critical; and it may be fairly argued, I think, that no other composer has destroyed so much of his own work or left to posterity so few routine works. Nevertheless, as we know, even Homer nodded; and it is with these choral works that Brahms nodded most of all.

The reasons, as I see it, are twofold: the first being the one I have already suggested, namely, his agnostic temperament war-

*Hans Gals, *Johannes Brahms* (London: Severn Publishers, 1975).

ring with his subject matter and so crippling his inspiration—a war that he won only once with the *Requiem*. The second, I believe, is that he fell into the error of setting old words to old music, music that reflected his prolonged disciplinary study not only of the works of Bach and Handel but of pre-Baroque composers such as Palestrina, Lassus, Schütz, and their contemporaries with the purpose of extending and enriching his composing techniques. While that study achieved its aim, it also had the deleterious effect when writing choral works of binding him in an archaic straight-jacket from which he never completely freed himself.

Examination of these works shows that it was not technique that handicapped him and made them lackluster and devoid of character, since they are full of intricate and skillful examples of fugue, canon, imitation, harmony, and all the rest of compositional technique. What in modern parlance fails to make them tick and seem alien to the composer's natural idiom is—to repeat—the error of setting the archaic words in an archaic style. Now, I maintain that the only way for a modern composer to set old words is to new music: by which I mean in the composer's natural contemporary style as Schubert and Finzi, for example, did for Shakespeare, and Britten did for Michelangelo, and for the classic poems of his *Serenade*. Transmuted in this way, old words not only retain their old life but attain a new one. To set them in the mode of their own period is to do what student painters do when copying an old masterpiece, namely, produce mere imitation. This is what Brahms did, I opine, in these works. Archaic, imitative, obsolescent, and mimetic, they are only skillful copies of the genuine Mona Lisa. Or as Brahms himself confessed almost agonizingly in a letter (1872) to his beloved Clara: "I have been studying counterpoint the whole winter. Why? . . . I hardly know. There is certainly an element of tragedy in becoming in the end too clever for one's needs." Which puts what I have written in a nutshell.

10

The Major Choral Works

To leave the preceding minor works for the major ones is, with one notable exception, to meet the composer of the chamber, symphonic, and piano masterpieces.

This single exception, *Rinaldo* (Op. 50) happens to have come into being more or less contemporaneously with the *Requiem*, and only slightly before the *Liebeslieder*, the *Alto Rhapsody*, and the *Song of Destiny*, three of the composer's most inspired works. Begun and finished in 1863 (except for the final chorus, not added until 1868) while the *Requiem* was slowly formulating in his mind and being spasmodically written down, *Rinaldo* is probably the result of Brahms's thoughts of turning to opera, since we know that at this time he was looking at one or two possible libretti. This essay in the objective and dramatic may well have been made as a preliminary sortie into that arena. If so, it must be admitted that the choice of this Goethe text was unfortunate, lacking as it does any sense of drama. In addition, the story of the enchantress, Armida, and her spellbound lover, Rinaldo, taken from Tasso's *La Gerusalemme Liberata*, had already been used by Lully, Gluck, Haydn, and by Handel in the first of his London operas.

Brahms's setting of the Goethe text is scored for tenor solo, men's chorus, and orchestra, and consists mainly of antiphonal correlation between solo and chorus, in which the latter (the sailors) keep trying to persuade Rinaldo (solo) to break the amorous spell of the enchantress and to leave the island. But just as in the unsatisfactory text Armida does not utter a word, so in Brahms's musical interpretation she never so much as puts in an appearance, thus losing any possible dramatic core in the situation to begin with.

Finally, to add to this inherent weakness, the music confesses that unlike Handel, Mozart, Weber, and Verdi, but along with Schubert and Mendelssohn, Brahms was unable to adjust his style to different poetic subjects—a fact already evinced by the *Magelone Romances*. As with Schubert in his operas, Brahms, similarly lyrical and introspective, lacked that instinct of timing and proportion to be found in all the great operatic composers. For example, in his opera *Alcina*, Handel sets the farewell scene of the enchantress to her magic island in a five-minute stroke of genius with the superb aria *Verdi prati*, and it is all that is needed. Here in *Rinaldo*, expressing a similar situation, it takes Brahms fifty lines of text and nearly a thousand bars of aria. The result is too long and too flaccid and becomes a bore. The finest episode in the work is the final sailors' chorus (added five years later) in which, freed from his dramatic trapping, the composer was able to give rein to his subjective lyricism. One can only adjudge from the work that had Brahms ever attempted opera the result would not have been a success.

With the *Ein Deutches Requiem* we come to the first of the composer's choral masterworks, and one which, moreover, along with his first piano concerto and symphony, was to give him the most trouble in its composition and fears in performance.

Some commentators have presumed that it was the deaths of his mentor, Schumann, in such tragic circumstances, and later of his mother, that drove him into composing the Requiem. True, he had loved them both dearly, and no doubt the loss of them must have deepened his sense of despair and need of consolation. But such was the innate melancholy of his nature that he might well have eventually written such a work apart from and above personal feelings. Earlier works such as the *Funeral Hymn*, the *Sacred Song*, certain of the more somber lieder, the *Song of Destiny*, *Nänie*, and *Song of the Fates* betray his preoption for the themes of human destiny and death. And in fact he was known later to have declared that the work was a Requiem for all humanity rather than a personal In Memoriam.

But at least it may be said, I think, that the deaths of his mother and of Schumann, along with his own nature, drove him into its composition if for no other reason than as a desperate attempt to exorcise his grief through the artist's act of creation. The D-minor piano concerto and the C-minor piano quartet are other examples.

Now, the first observation needing to be made in any study of the Requiem is on the composer's choice of text, for without understanding the reasons for the choice no full comprehension of the work is possible. To Brahms, with his North German Lutheran upbringing, allied with his later agnosticism, the liturgical text of the Catholic Mass, with its tenets of purgatory, salvation, and resurrection was utterly aesthenic and alien for him, and impossible to set. His disbelief allowed no penitential breast-beating, no histrionic Miserere or Dies Irae. His philosophy was expressed in the lines he had written to his beloved Clara after the death of his mother: "There is nothing to be altered, nothing to regret for a sensible man. It is simply a matter of carrying on and keeping one's head above water."*

He therefore carefully selected biblical words that avoided religious dogma but, while accepting death as a function of nature and inevitable, at least gave some human consolation. To underscore this fact, he based his texts not on the usual Latin Mass but, perhaps with Schubert's German Masses in mind, on those of Luther's translation of the bible, and he deliberately and combatatively styled the work Ein Deutches Requiem, adding after the title the plausible Nach Worten der heiliger Schrift (According to the words of Holy Scripture)—plain indication that he was not using orthodox text. And he even went to the length of telling Reinthaler, organist at Bremen cathedral who gave the first full performance there, that he would have liked to call it a "Requiem for Mankind."

It is not surprising, therefore, that the harassed composer had premonitions of contest over the work, premonitions proving only too well-founded. His choice of text alone served to antagonize certain critics, who refused to accept it as a Requiem and dubbed it "a sacred cantata," "a funeral chant," a "so-called religious work devoid of creed," and so on, seemingly unable to accept the fact that Brahms, like any other composer, chose texts that responded to his own feelings.

*Geiringer, Brahms: His Life and Work.

The texts he finally came to set, all taken from the Lutheran Bible, were:

1. *Selig sind, die das Leid tragen* (Blessed are they that mourn. Psalm 126).
2. *Denn alles Fleisch es ist wie Gras* (For all flesh is grass. Peter, James, Isaiah).
3. *Herr, lehre doch mich dass ein Ende* (Lord, make me to know mine end. Wisdom, Psalm 39).
4. *Wie lieblich sind deine Wohnungen* (How lovely are thy dwellings. Psalm 84).
5. *Ihr habt nun Traurigkeit* (And ye now, therefore, have sorrow. John, Isaiah, Ecclesiastes).
6. *Denn wir haben hier keine bleibende Statt* (For here we have no abiding city. Corinthians, Revelations).
7. *Selig sind die Todten die dem Herren sterben* (Blessed are the Dead who die in the Lord. Revelations).

As can be seen at once from these, Brahms was a man in desperate need of comfort, and pathetically seeking it from the Book he knew so well; and in that state of mind he began the search for it by translating the words in terms of music as early as 1857–59* by adapting a projected but finally rejected slow movement for his D-minor piano concerto as a setting of "All flesh is grass," eventually to become the second movement of the Requiem. And it was at this time that personal circumstances helped to influence his choice of text. Following his mother's death in 1856, he became restless and unable to settle in any one place—a state inducing him to select "But here we have no abiding city" for the sixth movement.

The first version of the work was finally completed in 1866 while Brahms was holidaying in Switzerland. I say "first version" because for its first public performance in Vienna on December 1st of the following year, given by the Gesellschaft der Musikfreunde under Herbeck as part of a concert given in memory of Schubert, the work consisted of only three movements. Moreover, that performance was as little successful as that of the D-minor piano concerto, due to two factors: under-rehearsal, the

---

*"The German Requiem . . . . occupied him at intervals for upwards of ten years." Geiringer, *Brahms: His Life and Work.*

over-enthusiasm of the tympanist, who completely drowned out the rest of the orchestra during the long pedal D of the final fugue in the third movement; and the G♭ section of the second movement, at the words "So seid nun geduldig," which in its faster and lighter 3/4 meter resembled, so the more critical of its listeners averred, a Viennese ländler, and as such is ludicrously misplaced. Brahms saw that the first fault lay partly in the orchestration, which he not only rescored, but also went on to add a fourth movement. But he did nothing about the offending quasi-ländler! Yet still he was not finished with the work. For the official and all-important performance in Bremen cathedral during the Easter of 1868, carefully rehearsed by Carl Reinthaler, he added yet another two movements. This time its success was unquestioned. But it was only after this and for another performance in Leipzig nearly a year later that he added the lovely soprano solo to give the work its final complement of seven movements.

Movement 1

The text and history considered, let us turn to the music itself. For the first half of the opening movement Brahms banishes the violins and clarinets and subdivides the violas and cellos, thus giving the episode a timbre of gloom expressive of the text—Blessed are they that mourn.

Ex. 89 *Requiem,* Movement 1

Not until the modulation into D♭ at bar 47 does the chorus swing into quicker movement and brighter expression. But this scarcely gets under way when the lugubrious Fmajor theme returns with the four voices in imitation. After 15 bars this in turn makes a reprise to the pivotal D♭, and it is in the course of these 18 bars that for the first time a sense of consolation emerges.

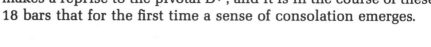

Ex. 90 *Requiem,* Movement 1

Movement 2

It was this movement which, rescued from its originally projected place in the D minor piano concerto, caused no little comment on the part of critics. This was not only because it was
designated as being in the style of a march in 3/4 meter and in
the lugubrious key of B♭ minor, but also because after running
its funereal way for 74 bars, it incongruously changed its tempo,
key and character to become faster and suspiciously like a ländler, to the outrage of not a few of its first hearers. Today one
commentator at least can only agree with those contemporary
critics and state bluntly that the episode is an undeniable lapse,
not so much on account of its ländler character (after all, the
words call for something brighter) as because its square rhythm,
elementary sequences, and hymnal harmonies make it a neutral
incongruity in an otherwise splendid movement.

Movement 3

The text of the third movement is superlatively expressed in
the D minor baritone solo with which it opens. In its pensive
eloquence, its tessitura and its static chordal accompaniment it
suggests a futuristic look to the *Four Serious Songs.* After sixteen
bars of the solo the chorus enters, repeating the words and melody of the solo in simple diatonic harmony, then giving way in
turn to the solo voice, which is again echoed by the choir. Finally,
after a brief episode in the major closing on a dominant chord,
the tenors launch themselves into the subject of the fugue sung
through its full length over a pedal D—that notorious *pedal* ru-
ined by the tympanist at the work's first public performance—
to bring the movement to a close of incomparable grandeur.

Ex. 91 *Requiem*, Movement 3

Movement 4

After three such movements of storm and stress, Brahms must have sensed that some relief was necessary; so, giving rein to his lyrical genius, he gives us *Wie lieblich sind deine Wohnungen* (How lovely are thy dwellings), a number that comes like an oasis in a harrowing landscape. This, with its lesser demand on voice and orchestra has made it the most frequently performed and best known number of the work. The movement is not only wonderfully expressive in its wistful pathos, but superbly constructed and orchestrated. The initial rising phrase from the cellos against the downward moving woodwind may be said to epitomise the movement in its delicate orchestral tracery and its expression of hopeful resignation

Ex. 92 *Requiem*, Movement 4

Movement 5

The fifth movement was the last to be added to the work, and as stated earlier, the text, with its reference to a mother comforting her children, may well have occurred to Brahms following his mother's death. How right he was to give the solo to a soprano voice. The number is not only movingly expressive but superbly shaped and orchestrated. The opening phrase, rising on muted strings, becomes the core of the movement, taken over now by the voice, now by the woodwinds, now by the violins, and passing through several modulations.

Ex. 93 *Requiem*, Movement 5

It may seem pointless to pick out specific instances when the whole is one radiance, but the closing bars of the solo's *Ich will euch wieder sehen* above the chorus's *Ich will euch trösten*, with its bare orchestral support and especially the horns' low octaves followed by *tenuto* strings and the ethereal soaring of the woodwinds, is surely one of the most moving closes in all music.

Ex. 94 *Requiem*, **Movement 5**

Movement 6

Following the final G-major chord of the preceding number, this movement, although in C minor, by way of introduction repeats the chorus with muted strings to be answered in D minor by flutes, oboes, clarinets, and horns. There the chorus enters in simple four-part choral style in a series of triads and to a marchlike rhythm emphasized by pizzicato bass strings.

Ex. 95 *Requiem*, Movement 6

This serves as a twenty-eight bar introduction to the baritone solo, which enters with the words made familiar to British ears by *Messiah*: "Siehe, ich sage euch ein Geheimnis' (Behold, I tell you a mystery), announced quasi-recitativo over a timpani roll. After a modulation into F♯ minor, the solo continues in that key, to be echoed by the chorus. Only with the advent of the words "zu der Zeit der letzen Posaune" (at the time of the last trumpet), and the ensuing return to the key of E♭, does the music rouse itself from its mood of quiescence to erupt into an apocalyptic *vivace*, with the full orchestral panoply of trumpets, tuba, trombones, and strings. This episode, after being interrupted by a brief solo from the baritone, is continued for a triumphant seventy-six bars, when, after a *ff* series of sustained chords from the chorus to a rising and falling orchestral bass, with a defiant plunge into the major, the altos begin the double fugue "Herr, du bist würdig" (Lord, thou art worthy). This continues for 130 bars over onrunning strings. The movement closes with monumental power and Handelian grandeur.

Ex. 96 *Requiem,* Movement 6

Ex. 97 *Requiem,* Movement 6

Movement 7

The final number reverts not only to the F major of the first, indicative of Brahms's classical architectonic instinct, but also concludes with thematic reference to it. The whole purpose of the number is to bring consolation to the bereaved, not from any divine source but from remembrance of the lives and works of those taken by death. It is the same catharsis as can be found again in *Nänie*.

The movement begins darkly, with a pedal F from the organ, and low upward tending notes first from the cellos, then from the violas and violins as if in entreaty, emphasized by the suppliant soprano entry at the second bar, answered later by the basses.

Ex. 98 *Requiem*, Movement 7

At bar 47, on the word 'Arbeit,' the music modulates caressingly into A major to introduce a 26-bar episode of interweaving voices over a rocking accompaniment of sextuplet quavers that convey the sense of restfulness imparted by the words.

Ex. 99 *Requiem*, Movement 7

This ends with a return to the tonic F major and the opening bars to form a perfect ending to the whole work, the music dying away in a mood of resignation and confidence. For Brahms, the ultimate climax of joy was quiet rapture.

Ex. 100 *Requiem,* **Movement 7**

With the *Requiem,* Brahms achieved four notable things: his first choral masterpiece; fame, in that it was only after its Bremen performance in 1868 and its publication later in the same year that his name began to be placed alongside those of his contemporaries, Liszt, Tchaikovsky, and Wagner; a mastery of orchestration, which prepared him for the choral works and first symphony soon to come; and finally, an incomparable and rare expression in terms of music of human genius and philosophy.

With *Schicksalslied* (Song of Destiny) for chorus and orchestra, we make a return to the secular Brahms. He was staying with his friend, Albert Dietrich, when, as the latter records* 'Early that morning he came across a copy of Hölderlin's poems in the book-case, and was deeply moved by the *Schicksalslied*.' The theme of the poem—the contrast between the bliss of the supposed 'blessed ones' in Elysium and the lot of mere mortals on earth with their unending struggle against Fate, or Destiny—naturally gripped the melancholy imagination of the composer. Yet, its composition gave him no little trouble; for after interpreting the happiness of the Elysian spirits and the troubled, thwarted lot of earth-bound mortals in terms of music, he found he could not bring himself to end with the poet's gloomy acceptance of hu-man fate. After much doubt and hesitation, he first followed the suggestion of Hermann Levi, his friend and the conductor of the Karlsrühe Opera House, and added an Epilogue in the shape of a choral setting of the poem's opening verses. But then his in-stinct told him that such a solution was wrong. After further hesitation, he substituted for it the *Adagio* it now has—all of which explains the time taken over the work, which, begun in 1868 soon after the *Requiem*, was not completed until May, 1871.

Certainly the care and thought taken over the work was well vindicated, for as we now have it, it is one of the composer's most original and profound. From the first bars, with their expressive scoring for woodwinds over the soft throbbing of the timpani coming through like heartbeats, it arrests attention.

*A. Dietrich, *Recollections of Johannes Brahms* (London: 1899).

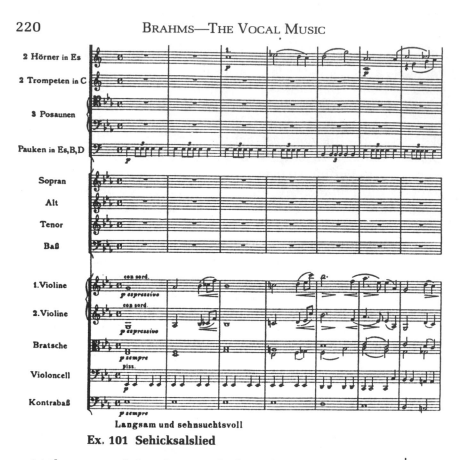

Ex. 101 Sehicksalslied

At the entry of the altos, with the sole exception of an E♭ held by cellos, the strings are silenced and the vocal line accompanied only by flute, oboe, clarinet, and horn—a stroke of musical imagination conveying the ethereal peace of the "blessed Spirits."

Ex. 102 Sehicksalslied

But this is only the first of similar felicities, the whole score being colored by innumerable other examples; the effect of repose conveyed by the transition from a p major 4/4 time to a virulent 3/4 *allegro* in the relative minor for the reentry of the chorus at *Doch uns ist gegeben*, expressing the grim contrasting state of mortals; woodwind *sotto voce* passages during intervals of a silenced choir; the febrile surges of the strings; the sinister unisons and wild outcries from chorus and orchestra at *wie Wasser von Kippe*. And finally, after the frenzy of this episode has died down to a resigned pp, the orchestra restates the wonderful C-minor prelude, only now rescored in the major; and with an ethereal upward shifting of horns, clarinets, and flutes, the movement ends on a hushed C-major chord. This *Adagio* is so moving and makes such a crowning glory to the work that I quote it in full. Study of it should dispel the notion that Brahms was an indifferent orchestrator.

Ex. 103 Sehicksalslied

The Rhapsody, for contralto, men's chorus, and orchestra, was composed in the autumn of 1869 after the *Song of Destiny*, and here indeed one senses a melancholy state of mind. I have already touched on the reasons for this in my reference to the *Liebeslieder*. We learn of the background to the work's composition from a moving passage in Clara's diary, concerning her daughter's future:

> Julie bears the uncertainty of her fate with exemplary patience, and she is always sweet and attentive to me . . . At last there came Marmorito's formal proposal, and on Sunday I wrote him my consent, but God knows my heart bled as I wrote . . . Of course I told Johannes first of all. He seemed not to have expected anything of the sort, and to be quite upset . . . Johannes is quite altered. He seldom comes to the house and speaks only in monosyllables when he does. And he treats Julie in the same way, though he always used to be specially nice to her. Did he really love her?*

And later we are told that on Julie's wedding day Brahms turned up at the house with the manuscript of the work, referring to it bitterly as his "bridal song." And Clara adds: "It is long since I was so moved by a work revealing such depths of despair by both words and music."

In this respect the *Rhapsody* could stand as a perfect illustration of the Goethe poem with which the *Neue Liebeslieder* ends, with its theme that the Muses cannot completely cure the anguish of a lover's despondent heart though they may impart some comfort and consolation. In the full flood of hope Brahms wrote the *Liebeslieder*; in the full flood of heartache the *Rhapsody*. Goethe's poem *Harzreise im Winter* contrasts the contentedness of the gregarious huntsmen and other denizens of the forest with the unhappiness of the lonely misanthrope who happens to come across them in the course of his solitary wanderings, and concludes with a nebulous prayer to the "Vater der Liebe" to bestow some consoling benediction on this hater of human kind. While to an alien aesthetic the poem may seem enigmatic and pretentious in its Teutonic pseudo-religious philosophy, its three central stanzas were seized on by Brahms as being expressive of his own emotions, at least at that moment, and he made the most of them. The embittered loneliness of the self-doomed outcast is vividly caught in the dissonant eighteen-bar orchestral prelude, with its muted violins, *sforzando tremolos*, low-pitched basses, and eerie tone of blended horn and bassoon.

*Karl Geiringer, *Brahms: His Life and Work*.

Rhapsodie

(Fragment aus Goethes Harzreise im Winter)

für eine Altstimme, Männerchor und Orchester

Ex. 104 *Rhapsody* for contralto, men's chorus and orchestra

The voice enters, accompanied by strings, as in the prelude, sounding like distant thunder. This C-minor episode, closing on a *tenuto* dominant chord, leads into the *poco andante*, in which the voice declaims the next stanza *Ach, wer heilet die Schmerzen* with a typical Brahms melody not only in its warm lyricism but also in its cross-rhythm of 3/2 and 6/4, giving the effect of the solitary wanderer stumbling uncertainty along.

Ex. 105 *Rhapsody* **for contralto, men's chorus and orchestra**

Words and melody are then repeated, differently orchestrated, to lead after sixty-eight bars into the final *Adagio*, transposed by an inspired stroke into the major and 4/4 meter. Cellos illustrate the line *Ist auf deinem Psalter, Vater der Liebe* in harplike *pizzicato* to the voice's glorious melody, now at last accompanied by the chorus and textured by ethereal flutes, clarinets, bassoons, and horns.

Ex. 106 *Rhapsody* for contralto, men's chorus and orchestra

The work ends in poignant resignation, with scoring for the two horns and violas.

Ex. 107 *Rhapsody* for contralto, men's chorus, and orchestra

Was Brahms the indifferent orchestrator some critics maintain he is, one asks? Only 168 bars in length, the *Rhapsody* is one of the most concentrated and moving examples of intellectual and emotional inspiration in the annals of music.

The trio of masterworks, Opps. 52, 53, and 54, just failed to be continued with Op. 55, the *Triumphlied*. The incentive for the composition of this Song of Triumph came from the strong, even overstrong, patriotism of the composer and his jubilation at the

German victories over the French, whom he disliked, in the Franco-Prussian war of 1870–71, by which his hero, Bismarck,* achieved the unification of Germany and had the Prussian King Wilhelm IV, declared emperor as Kaiser Wilhelm I. So, just as Handel had celebrated the victory of the English over the French with his *Dettingen Te Deum*, in emulation Brahms decided to compose his own celebration, and doing so grandiloquently with a work for eight-part chorus, baritone solo, and orchestra. Like Handel, he chose the text for setting himself, selecting the nineteenth chapter of Revelations, celebrating the triumph over the "Whore of Babylon," doubtless symbolic in the composer's eyes of the fall of Paris to German arms.

For us today, such a text can only seem as nauseatingly despotic as "Land of Hope and Glory" with the belief in divine-granted support for their countries' expansionist aims; but in extenuation it must be borne in mind that Brahms, like Elgar after him, really believed in the sacredness of his country's cause, and was therefore able to give free rein to his patriotic exultation. And exult Brahms certainly does. Critics one and all have admired the work's brilliant orchestration, its contrapuntal deftness, its masterly handling of the two four-part choirs, now in antiphony, now in intricate counterpoint, and its blazing fanfares and hallelujahs. All of which reads like an unreserved paean of praise. But underneath all the technical brilliance, one has a niggling doubt as to the intrinsic worth of the music. Like Handel's Coronation Anthems and Te Deums (and of all Brahms's works *Triumphlied* most reflects the influence of Handel), it makes splendid ceremonial music, but is grandiose rather than great, magniloquent rather than puristic, so that one hesitates to place it on the heights of the preceding introspective, less brilliant but more profound masterpieces.

As further evidence of his patriotic fervor, Brahms dedicated the work to the new Emperor of Germany. As a postscript to our discussion of the opus, it is perhaps worthwhile relating that after hearing a performance of it in Karlsrühe in June, 1872, by his friend, Hermann Levi, he began to have misgivings as to its propriety, now that the war that inspired it was over, and even expressed a wish that there should be no further performances—

*On all his wanderings Brahms invariably carried a copy of Bismarck's speeches in his travel bag.

which did not prevent it from being acclaimed everywhere throughout Germany.

*　*　*

A decade was to pass before the composition of the next choral work with orchestra, namely *Nänie*. The first thing any commentator must do is to explain the somewhat strange title and the background against which the composer wrote it, since without that knowledge it must lose much of its significance. Nänie, Naenia, or Nenia, was the name given in ancient Rome to the funeral songs women, called Praeficae, sang. Nänie is, then, a threnody, and its origins spring from the fact that while spending the summer of 1864 at Clara Schumann's cottage in Lichtental, Brahms met and became friendly with celebrities such as Turgenief, Anton Rubinstein, Johann Strauss, and the neoclassic painter, Anselm Feuerbach. And it was the sad, comparatively early death in 1880 of Feuerbach that impelled the composer to write his funeral tribute, based on Schiller's poem— an elegy on the inevitable end of all humanity, young or old, high or low, commonplace or genius. All beauty perishes, and our only consolation must be in our songs of mourning for the lost loved ones and the memories they leave with us is, as with the *Requiem*, the core of the poet's theme. Such a one, as we know, always held Brahms's sympathies. Scored for mixed chorus and orchestra, the work spans no more than 180 bars, and in its concentrated, emotive power links itself with those similar masterworks, the *Alto Rhapsody* and the *Song of Destiny*, nor does it suffer in comparison.

The twenty-four-bar orchestral prelude, with its *pizzicato* strings throbbing beneath wind instruments, and its haunting oboe melody, creates the solemn atmosphere of the memorial tribute.

Ex. 108 *Nänice*

The voices enter in a p *fugato*. The reference to Aphrodite rising from the sea to mourn for her son Achilles (as usual, Schiller's poem is full of classical allusions) brings in the harp. After twenty-five bars we are led from the tonic D major key to a *più sostenuto* in F♯ major magically scored by the harp plucking rising quaver triplets against the strings' duple quavers, wreathing the music in a delicate tracery of string-and-harp figuration, while the chorus, after three bars of unison, sings a chorale-like theme.

Ex. 109 Nänie

From this, a reprise is made to the opening section, showing that Brahms, even in his most romantic works, instinctively thought in terms of classical sonata form. Significantly, for the closing bars he threw out the poem's grim final line declaring that the unworthy descend into the Underworld unsung, choosing instead to finish with the consolatory penultimate line "Auch ein Klaglied zu sein im Mund der Geliebten ist herrlich," the final "herrlich" being repeated three times before dying away in its own quiet beauty.

Ex. 110 *Nänie*

Thoughtfully for once, Brahms dedicated the work to the painter's widow.

The last of the major choral works followed in the summer of 1882 while the composer was staying at Ischl, and was dedicated to Duke Georg II. The reason for the dedication was the fact that his friend and admirer, von Bülow, who had given the first performance of the C-minor symphony in Hanover, had obtained the congenial post of Music Director at the music-loving ducal court of Meiningen and, always keen to forward Brahms's cause, the pianist-conductor had taken advantage of his status to introduce the composer into the court circles there. Feeling honored by the great man's presence in their midst, duke and duchess and their entourage fussed over him to his heart's content, and in gratitude Brahms dedicated his latest work to the duke.

The composition in question was the *Gesang der Parzen* (Song of the Fates), suggested by a performance Brahms had heard in Vienna of Goethe's classical *Iphigenia*. From the play he selected six stanzas from the fourth act—a passage in which Iphigenia relates her childhood memories of hearing the Song of the Fates. There is little doubt, however, that Brahms took Goethe's stanzas acknowledging the pitiless power of fate over human destinies as being not only personal to himself but to all humanity, thus making its theme similar to that of the earlier *Schicksalslied*. While its 176 bars make it much the same length as the *Rhapsody* and *Nänie*, it cannot in toto stand beside them as one of the composer's masterpieces. The main reason for this lies in its lack of rhythmic variety (for which Goethe's verses are partly to blame, being depressingly monochrome), a fact that, despite its brevity, makes it seem monotonously lugubrious. To begin with, the chorus, scored for SAATBB, tends to be bottom-heavy. Then, after a somber orchestral prelude of nineteen bars in a *ff* D minor, creating an atmosphere of menace and giving the listener anticipation of another *Song of Destiny*, Brahms can do little except repeat the subject, first by the male then by the female voices in two-bar phrases, then again in four-bar phrases, after which the full choir continues for thirty-eight bars in chorale-like homophony—a style that pervades the work, yielding little variety. Though there are changes of key (to C♯ minor and D major) there is no change in the slow tempo, causing the whole work to sound gloomily static. As usual, for a coda Brahms makes a return to the opening D-minor subject, ending *perdendosi* in a ppp close.

In justice, and countering the general unfavorable criticism, it should be stated that these last sixteen bars are the highlight of the work, constituting in their highly original, orchestration,

Ex. 111 *Gesang der Parzen*

rhythmic subtlety, and harmonic color one of the most astonishing passages in nineteenth-century music.

I conclude my review of Brahms's vocal works with the Op. 91 *2 Songs for Contralto, Viola, and Piano*, placed apart in lonely splendor in that it falls into no category, being neither lieder nor choral, and is the only one of its kind.

The story behind its inception is as fascinating as the songs themselves. Among the composer's greatest admirers and longest held friends were the famous violinist Joseph Joachim (for whom he wrote his Violin Concerto) and his wife, Amalie Weiss, opera singer for whom he wrote the *Alto Rhapsody*. It was therefore with deep sadness that in the early 1880s he learned that their marriage was on the point of breaking up due to the violinist's constant morbid jealousy, culminating in unfounded accusations of her being unfaithful to him. So distressed, in fact, was Brahms, that he wrote a letter of sympathy, which, to quote Geiringer, "is unique in the whole of Brahms's correspondence for its length and warmth of tone."* Not only so, but in a despairing effort to bring the estranged pair together once more, he wrote these songs, giving each a performing part in the hope that by their sharing in the music-making the breach might be healed. The anecdote reveals a tenderness and compassion in the composer's nature too rarely expressed and for which he has been given little credence.

To come to the songs themselves. For *Gestille Sehnsucht*, the first of the two, Brahms chose for his text a poem of Rückert's depicting a contrast between "a golden evening" in the heart of the countryside with the restlessness of his feelings, and as Geiringer again so aptly observes, Brahms's setting reveals once again his deep love of nature. The soft viola arpeggios magically portray the light rustle of the breeze, and voice, viola, and piano vie with one another in creating a superb musical interpretation of the poem.

For the *Geistliches Wiegenlied*, Brahms took for his text Geibel's translation of a poem from the *Spanisches Liederbuch* depicting Mary lulling her son to sleep. Seizing on the fact that it was a cradle song, very aptly Brahms took over the melody of an old, well-known German cradle song and made it the theme for a lovely 6/8 rocking *cantilena*, giving the viola a *canto firmus* against rich, soft harmonies from the voice and piano. Like that of Schubert's and his own famous *Wiegenlied*, this is yet another magical cradle song enriching the singer's treasury.

*Geiringer, *Brahms: His Life and Work*.

Postlude

After any review of Brahms's vocal works it becomes all but impossible not to ask oneself why, when the dead wood has been taken out (and there is a good deal of that, as I have admitted) but with so many masterpieces still remaining, so few are ever performed and consequently so little known even to musicians. The answer is to be found, I believe, on two fronts, namely, the domestic and the public; that is, the amateur and the professional.

To take the former first. A clue to the puzzle lies in the composer's own words to his publisher, Simrock, on the eve of the publication of the *Liebeslieder Waltzer*: "Let us hope they will become real family music, and sung a lot." And in fact his hopes were fulfilled, for the work soon came to be among his best loved and most widely performed—at least in his lifetime and in German-speaking countries. I cannot speak for those countries, but today in our own, alas, it has to be confessed that family music-making has all but disappeared, strangled by radio and television. Anyone now can bring into the home music performed by world-famous professionals, which is why the violinist Fritz Kreisler refused to broadcast. To him, audience presence and participation were essential for the creation and performance of his unique art. But modern mechanical expertise seems to have made those factors unnecessary to the majority of today's music lovers. Why go to the trouble of making music oneself when it can be heard professionally and better at the turning of a knob? Before these inventions came into being, one heard and read of German and Austrian households making music an essential part of their existence, and of servants in wealthy establishments singing folk songs and even Schubert as they went about their work. Where is that background now? Gone, it is to be feared, with the snows of yesteryear.

This deplorable state of affairs means the disappearance from the general scene of so much wonderful music, both vocal and instrumental, as, for example, the trio sonatas and Italian duetti of Handel, the piano duets of Mozart and Schubert, the whole corpus of madrigals, the part-songs of Schubert, Schumann, Mendelssohn, and Franz, among which are to be found some of the most attractive music ever committed to paper.

It is precisely into this vacuum that Brahms's Chorlieder fall.

On the professional front, against which not only Brahms's vocal works but all such founder, is the state of the concert scene, in this country at least. To take lieder first. Even in the country of its birth and adoption, the lied is limited in its appeal, demanding as it does a knowledge, study, and concentration that confine appreciation to a minority. In this country the effort of listening to a song recital in German is understandably difficult. In addition, stemming from this and equally understandable, there is a dearth of lieder singers. In England we have had no Fischer-Dieskau, Peter Schrier, Elena Gerhardt, Elizabeth Schumann, or Ilse Wolf. And then, to finalize the subject, whenever a singer daringly gives a performance of lieder, bowing to audience pressure, his or her program will almost certainly consist of the handful of better-known songs. For these reasons, something like ninety percent of Brahms's lieder have never been sung on English concert platforms.

To come finally to the chorlieder—that is to say the chamber ensembles and smaller choral works. Here, in addition to the dearth of amateur music-making we are brought up against present-day professional concert fashions. Disregarding opera, the only choral works to enjoy live public performance seem to be those of suitable length to fill an evening: works, for example, such as those of a Handel, Haydn, Mendelssohn, or Elgar Oratorio, a Bach Passion, a Haydn Mass, or the Verdi or Fauré Requiem. How often do concert promotors and conductors have the idea of putting on a group of shorter works. How many times can we hope to hear live performances of, say, a Purcell Masque, the *Dixit Dominus, Acis & Galatea, Te Deums* or *Chandos Anthems* of Handel, a cantata of Bach, the Haydn or Bruckner *Te Deums,* the *Nuits d'Été* of Berlioz, or the *Oedipus Rex* and *Symphony of*

Psalms of Stravinsky, to name only a few masterworks that spring to mind?

And it is this nullification that prevents the similar works of Brahms from being performed. Of his choral works only the *Requiem*, being of requisite length, can claim any popularity, while other masterpieces like the *Song of Destiny*, *Nänie*, *Alto Rhapsody*, and the vocal quartets are left out of reckoning and to the mercy of radio and recording for performance. And there would appear to be no answer to the grotesque dilemma until the whole conception of our program planning is changed. And that, sadly, is as unlikely ever to arrive as the proverbial Greek Kalends.

But let there be no mistake over the issue. The fault lies with us, not with Brahms.

Appendix: Catalog of Works

I. Solo Songs for Voice and Piano

Opus	Title	Composed	Published	Text
3	*6 Songs for High Voice*	1852–53	1854	
	Liebestreu			Reinick
	Liebe und Frühling I, II			Fallersleben
	Lied			Bodenstedt
	In der Fremde			Eichendorff
	Lied			Eichendorff
6	*6 Songs for High Voice*	1852–53	1853	
	Spanisches Lied			Heyse
	Der Frühling			J. B. Rousseau
	Nachwirkung			Meissner
	Juche!			Reinick
	Wie die Wolke			Fallersleben
	Nachtigallen schwingen			Fallersleben
7	*6 Songs for Solo Voice*	1851–53	1854	
	Treue Liebe			Ferrand
	Parole			Eichendorff
	Anklänge			Eichendorff
	Volkslied			Trad.
	Die Trauernde			Trad.
	Heimkehr			Uhland
14	*8 Songs and Romances*	1858	1861	
	Vor dem Fenster			Trad.
	Vom verwundeten Knaben			Trad.
	Murrays Ermordung			From the Scottish
	Ein Sonett			Thibault
	Trennung			Trad.
	Gang zur Liebsten			Trad.
	Ständchen			Trad.
	Sehnsucht			Trad.

19	5 Lyrics	1858	1862	
	Der Kuss			Hölty
	Scheiden und Meiden			Uhland
	In der Ferne			Uhland
	Der Schmied			Uhland
	An eine Äolsharfe			Mörike
32	9 Songs and Melodies	1864	1864	
	Wie rafft' ich mich auf			v. Platen
	Nicht mehr zu dir			Daumer
	Ich schleich umher			v. Platen
	Der Strom, der neben mir			v. Platen
	Wehe, so willst du mich			v. Platen
	Du spricht, dass ich mich			v. Platen
	Bitteres zu sagen			Daumer
	So stehn wir			Daumer
	Wie bist du, meine Königin			Daumer
33	(15) Romances from Magelone	1–4, 1861 5/6, 1862 7–15, 1863–69	1865 1869	Tieck
43	4 Songs	1866–68	1868	
	Von ewiger Liebe			Wenzig
	Die Mainacht			Hölty
	Ich schell' mein Horn			Old German
	Das Lied vom H. von Falkenstein			Volkslied
46	4 Songs	1859–66	1868	
	Die Kränze			Daumer
	Magyarisch			Daumer
	Die Schale der Vergessenheit			Hölty
	An die Nachtigall			Hölty
47	5 Songs	1858–68	1868	
	Botschaft			Daumer
	Liebesglut			Daumer
	Sonntag			Volkslied
	O Liebliche Wangen			Flemming
	Die Liebende schreibt			Goethe
48	7 Songs	1855–68	1868	
	Der Gang zum Liebchen			From the Czech
	Der Uberläufer			Des Knaben Wunderhorn
	Liebesklage des Mädchens			Des Knaben Wunderhorn
	Gold überwiegt die Liebe			From the Czech

	Vergangen ist mir Glück und Heil			Old German
	Herbstgefühl			Schack
49	5 Songs	1864–68	1868	
	Am Sonntag Morgen			Heyse
	An ein Veilchen			Hölty
	Sehnsucht			Czech
	Wiegenlied			Wunderhorn/ Scherer
	Abenddämmerung			Schack
57	8 Songs and Ballads	1871	1871	Daumer
	Von waldbekränzter Höhe			
	Wenn du nur zuweilen lächelst			
	Es träumte mir			
	Ach, wende diesen Blick			
	In meiner Nächte Sehnen			
	Strahlt zuweilen			
	Die Schnur, die Perle an Perle			
	Unbewegte laue Luft			
58	8 Songs and Melodies	1868–71	1871	
	Blinde Kuh			Italian
	Während des Regens			Kopisch
	Die Spröde			Calabrian
	O komme, holde Sommer- nacht			Grohe
	Schwermut			Candidus
	In der Gasse			Hebbel
	Vorüber			Hebbel
	Serenade			Schack
59	8 Songs and Ballads	1871–73	1873	
	Dämmerung senkte sich von oben			Goethe
	Auf dem See ("Blauer Himmel")			Simrock
	Regenlied			Groth
	Nachklang			Groth
	Agnes			Mörike
	Eine gute, gute Nacht			Daumer
	Mein wundes Herz			Groth
	Dein blaues Auge			Groth
63	9 Songs and Ballads	1873–74	1874	
	Frühlingstrost			Schenkendorf
	Erinnerung			Schenkendorf

	An ein Bild			Schenkendorf
	An die Tauben			Schenkendorf
	Meine Liebe ist grun			Felix Schumann
	Wenn um den Hollunder			Felix Schumann
	Wie traulich war			Groth
	O wüsst ich doch			Groth
	Ich sah als Knabe			Groth
69	9 Songs	c. 1877	1877	
	Klage ("Ach mir fehlt")			Czech
	Klage ("O Felsen")			Slovak
	Abschied			Czech
	Des Liebsten Schwur			Czech
	Tambourliedchen			Candidus
	Vom Strande			Spanish
	Über die See			Lemcke
	Salome			Keller
	Mädchenfluch			Serbian
70	4 Songs	1875–77	1877	
	Im Garten am Seegestade			Lemcke
	Lerchengesang			Candidus
	Serenate			Goethe
	Abendregen			Keller
71	5 Songs	c. 1877	1877	
	Es liebt sich so lieblich			Heine
	An den Mond			Simrock
	Geheimnis			Candidus
	Willst du, dass ich geh?			Lemcke
	Minnelied			Hölty
72	5 Songs	1875–77	1877	
	Alte Liebe			Candidus
	Sommerfäden			Candidus
	O kühler Wald			Brentano
	Verzagen			Lemcke
	Unüberwindlich			Goethe
84	5 Romances and Songs	1881–82	1882	
	Sommerabend			Schmidt
	Der Kranz			Schmidt
	In der Beeren			Schmidt
	Vergebliches Ständchen			Zuccalmaglio
	Spannung			Zuccalmaglio
85	6 Songs	1878–79	1882	
	Sommerabend			Heine
	Mondenschein			Heine
	Mädchenlied			Serbian

	Ade!			Czech
	Frühlingslied			Geibel
	In Waldeseinkamseit			Lemcke
86	*6 Songs for Low Voice*	1873–79	1882	
	Therese			Keller
	Feldeinsamkeit			Allmers
	Nachtwandler			Kalbeck
	Über die Haide			Storm
	Versunken			Felix Schumann
	Todessehen			Schenkendorf
94	*5 Songs for Low Voice*	1879–84	1884	
	Mit vierzig Jahren			Ruckert
	Steig auf, geliebter Schatten			Halm
	Mein Herz ist schwer			Geibel
	Sapphische Ode			Schmidt
	Kein Haus, keine Heimat			Halm
95	*7 Songs*	c. 1884	1884	
	Das Mädchen			Serbian
	Bei dir sind meine Gedanken			Halm
	Beim Abschied			Halm
	Der Jäger			Halm
	Vorschneller Schwur			Serbian
	Mädchenlied			Italian
	Schön war, das ich dir weihte			Daumer
96	*4 Songs*	1884	1886	
	Der Tod, das ist die kühle Nacht			Heine
	Wir wandelten			Daumer
	Es schauen die Blumen			Heine
	Meerfahrt			Heine
97	*6 Songs*	1885	1886	
	Nachtigall			Reinhold
	Auf dem Schiffe			Reinhold
	Entführung			Alexis
	Dort in den Weiden			Zuccalmaglio
	Komm bald			Groth
	Trennung			Serbian
103	8 Zigeunerlieder (See Quartets)	1887	1888	Hungarian
105	*5 Songs for Low Voice*	1886–88	1888	
	Wie Melodien zieht es mir			Groth
	Immer leise wird mein			Lingg

	Schlummer			
	Klage			Zuccalmaglio
	Auf dem Kirchhofe			Liliencron
	Verrat			Lemcke
106	5 Songs	1885–88	1889	
	Ständchen			Kugler
	Auf dem See			Reinhold
	Es hing der Reif			Groth
	Meine Lieder			Frey
	Ein Wanderer			Reinhold
107	5 Songs	1886–89	1889	
	An die Stolze			Flemming
	Salamander			Lemcke
	Das Mädchen spricht			Gruppe
	Maienkätzchen			Liliencron
	Mädchenlied			Heyse
121	Vier ernste Gesänge	1896	1896	Biblical
	Denn es gehet dem Menschen			
	Ich wandte mich			
	O Tod, wie bitter bist du			
	Wenn ich mit Menschen			
No Opus Number	Mondnacht	c. 1853	1854	Eichendorff
	Regenlied	c. 1864	1907	Groth
	5 Lieder der Ophilia	1873	1935	Shakespeare
	14 Volks-Kinderlieder	1858	1958	
	28 Deutsche Volkslieder	1858	1926	
	49 Deutsche Volkslieder	1894	1894	

II. Songs for More than One Voice with Piano Accompaniment

Duets

20	3 Duets	1858–60	1861	Herder
	Weg der Liebe (I,II)			
	Die Meere			
28	4 Duets	1860–62	1864	
	Die Nonne und der Ritter			Eichendorff
	Vor der Turr			Old German
	Es rauschet das Wasser			Goethe
	Der Jäger und sein Liebchen			Fallersleben

61	*4 Duets* Die Schwestern Klosterfräulein Phänomen Die Boten der Liebe	1873–74	1874	 Mörike Kerner Goethe Wenzig
66	*5 Duets* Klange (I,II) Am Strande Jägerlied Hut du dich!	1873–75	1875	 Groth Holty Candidus Des Knaben Wunderhorn
75	*4 Ballads and Romances* Edward Guter Rat So lass uns wandern Walpurgisnacht	1877–78	1878	 Scottish Des Knaben Wunderhorn Wenzig Alexis

Quartets

30	Geistlicheslied	1856	1864	Flemming
31	*3 Quartets* Wechsellied zum Tanze Neckereien Der Gang zum Liebchen	1859–63	1864	 Goethe Spanish Bohemian
42	*3 Gesänge* Abendständchen Vineta Darthula's Grabgesang	1859–61	1868	 Brentano Müller ?
52	*Liebeslieder Waltzer*	1868–69	1869	Daumer
64	*3 Quartets* An die Heimat Der Abend Fragen	1874	1874	 Sternan Schiller Daumer
65	*Neue Liebeslieder Waltzer*	1874	1875	Daumer/Goethe
92	*4 Quartets* O schöne Nacht Spätherbst Abendlied Warum?			 Daumer Allmers Hebbel Goethe
93b	*Tafellied* (for mixed choir and piano)	1884	1885	Eichendorff

103	8 Zigeuner Lieder (also arranged as solo songs)	1887	1888	Hungarian
	He! Zigeuner			
	Hochgetürmte Rimaflut			
	Wisst ihr, wenn mein Kindchen			
	Lieber Gott, due weisst			
	Brauner Bursche fürt zum Tanze			
	Röslein dreie in der Reihe			
	Kommt dir manchmal in den Sinn			
	Rote Abenwolken			
112	6 Quartets (nos. 3–6 Zigeuner Lieder)	1888–91	1891	
	Sehnsucht			Kluger
	Nachtens			Kluger
	Himmel strahlt os hell			Hungarian
	Rote Rosen			Hungarian
	Brennessel steht am Weges Rand			Hungarian
	Liebe Schwalbe			Hungarian

III. Works for Mixed Chorus and Orchestra

13	Begräbnisgesang	1859	1861	Weisse
45	Ein Deutsches Requiem	1857–68	1868	Biblical
54	Schicksalslied	1868–71	1871	Hölderlin
55	Triumphlied	1870–71	1872	Biblical
82	Nänie	1880–81	1882	Schiller
89	Gesang der Parzen	1882	1883	Goethe

IV. Works for Women's Chorus

12	Ave Maria	1858	1861	Liturgical
17	4 Songs	1860	1862	
	Es tönt ein voller Harfenklang			Ruperti
	Lied			Shakespeare
	Der Gartner			Eichendorff
	Gesang aus Fingal			Ossian

27	Psalm XIII	1859	1863	Biblical
37	*3 Geistliche Chöre* O bone Jesu Adoramus Regina Coeli	1859–63	1866	Liturgical
44	*12 Lieder und Romanzen* Minnelied Der Bräutigam Barcarole Fragen Die Müllerin Die Nonne Nun steh'n die Rosen Die Berge sind spitz Am Wildbach die Weiden Un gehst du über den 　Kirchhof Die Braut Marznacht	1859–63	1866	Voss Eichendorff Italian Slav. Chamisso Uhland Heyse Heyse Heyse Heyse Müller Uhland

V. Works for Men's Chorus

50	Rinaldo	1863–68	1869	Goethe
53	Rhapsody	1869	1869	Goethe

VI. Works for Mixed Choir

22	*Marienlieder* Der Englische Gruss Maria's Kirchgang Maria's Wallfahrt Der Jäger Ruf zur Maria Magdelana Maria's Lob	1859(?)	1862	Trad.
29	*2 Motets* Es ist das Heil Schaffe in mir Gott	1860	1864	Old German
41	*5 Lieder* Ich swing' mein Horn Freiwillige her!	1861–62	1867	Old German Lemcke

	Geleit			Lemcke
	Marschiren			Lemcke
	Gebt acht!			Lemcke
62	*7 Lieder*	1874	1874	
	Rosmarin			Des Knaben Wunderhorn
	Von alten Liebesliedern			Des Knaben Wunderhorn
	Waldesnacht			Heyse
	Dern Herzlein mild			Heyse
	All meine Herzgedanken			Heyse
	Es geht ein Wehen			Heyse
	Vergangen ist mir Glück			Old German
74	*2 Motets*			
	Warum ist das Licht?	1877	1879	Biblical
	O Heiland			
93a	*6 Lieder und Romanzen*	1883–84	1884	
	Der Bucklichte Fiedler			Volkslied
	Das Mädchen			Serbian
	O süsser Mai			Arnim
	Fahr' wohl			Ruckert
	Der Falke			Serbian
	Beherzigung			Goethe
104	*5 Choruses*	c. 1888	1888	
	Nachtwache I, II			Ruckert
	Letztes Glück			Kalbeck
	Verlorene Jugend			Wenzig
	Im Herbst			Groth
109	*Fest-und Gedensprüche*	1886–88	1890	Biblical
	Unsere Vater hofften auf dich			
	Wenn ein Starker			
	Wo ist ein so herrlich Volk?			
110	*3 Motets*	1889	1890	Biblical
	Ich aber bin eland			
	Ach arme Welt			
	Wenn wir in höchsten Nöten sein			
113	*13 Canons for female voices*	?	1891	
	Göttlicher Morpheus			Goethe
	Grausam erweist sich Amor			Goethe
	Schlad, Kindlein, schlaf			Volkslied
	Wille, wille will			Volkslied
	So lange Schönheit			Fallersleben

Wenn die Klange nah'n			Eichendorff
Ein Gems auf dem Stein			Eichendorff
An's Auge des Liebsten			Rückert
Leisie Töne der Brust			Rückert
Ich weiss nicht			Rückert
Wenn Kummer hätte			Rückert
Ein förmig ist der Liebe Gram			Rückert
Zy Rauch muss werden			Rückert
91 *2 Songs for Contralto, piano and viola*	1884	1884	
Gestille Sehnsucht			Rückert
Geistliches Wiegenlied			Spanisches Liederbuch

Selected Bibliography

Works devoted solely to Brahms's vocal music

Friedländer, Max. *Brahms's Lieder.* London: Oxford University Press, 1928.
Sams, Eric. *Brahms's Songs.* London: J. M. Dent, 1928; reprint, 1957.

Biographies and Studies of Brahms

Cardus, Neville. *Ten Composers.* London: Cape, 1947.
Dale, Kathleen. *A Concert Goer's Companion—Brahms.* London: Clive Bingley, 1970.
Dietrich, A. *Recollections of Johannes Brahms.* London, 1899.
Evans, Edison. *Historical, Descriptive, and Analytical Account of the Entire Works of Johannes Brahms.* London: Neeves, 1912–35.
Fuller-Maitland, J. A. *Johannes Brahms.* London: Methuen, 1911.
Gals, Hans. *Johannes Brahms.* London: Severn House, 1963.
Geiringer, Karl. *Brahms: His Life and Work.* London: Allen & Unwin, 1936.
Henschel, G. *Personal Recollections of Johannes Brahms.* Boston, 1907.
Jacobson, Bernard. *The Music of Johannes Brahms.* London: Tantivy Press, 1977.
James, Burnett. *Brahms—A Critical Study.* London: J. M. Dent, 1972.
Kalbeck, Max. *Johannes Brahms.* 8 vols. Berlin: Deutsche Brahms Gesellschaft, 1904–14.
Keys, Ivor. *Johannes Brahms.* London: Helm, 1989.
Latham, Peter. *Brahms.* London: Dent Master Musicians, 1948.
MacDonald, Malcolm. *Brahms.* London: Dent Master Musicians, 1990.
May, Florence. *The Life of Johannes Brahms.* London: Reeves, 1905; reprint, 1948.
Newman, Ernest. *From the World of Music.* London: Calder, 1956.
Niemann, Walter. *Brahms.* New York, Knopf, 1929.
Schauffler, R. *The Unknown Brahms, His Life, Character, and Work.* New York, Mead, 1933.

Brahms's Songs and Choral Music

Index of Works Other than Songs

General Index